What Others Are Saying Abou

"The Bible says that we are to be transformed by the renewing of our minds. David Carr's challenging book will help people to do exactly this as they focus again on what it is to be a Christian with the 'mind of Christ'. The book is full of testimonies of people who, under David's ministry, have moved on in their relationship with the Lord. It should be read by everybody!"

Reinhard Bonnke
Evangelist, Christ for All Nations

"David Carr's book is essential reading on a disturbing topic which most of us acknowledge, but which few know how to deal with. Like the author, I feel concerned about the renewing of my mind in order not to be conformed to this world by allowing myself to be squeezed into its mouldy-mould. David Carr writes out of a lifetime of wrestling with the renewing and protecting of the mind, with passion, clarity and conviction."

The Rt Revd Dr John Sentamu
Designate Archbishop of York

"At last, a book by David Carr. As an outstanding man he has a proven track record in leadership and ministry touching four decades. A lover of people, he is loved by many and the pages of his first book ooze with spiritual insight, theological integrity, common sense and practical advice, all wrapped up in genuine compassion."

Dr John Andrews
Senior Minister, New Life Christian Centre, Rotherham

"David Carr is a long-time friend of mine. He is a busy pastor with an incredible counseling schedule. I want to recommend his new book, *Staying Sane in a Crazy World*. There is nothing more important for a believer than learning how to renew and protect the mind. There is an incredible attack against our thoughts on a daily basis. David is giving us excellent insights in his new book that will help everyone who experiences this challenge. It's a good read and an excellent way to invest a few hours of your time."

Terry Law
World Compassion, USA

STAYING SANE
IN A CRAZY
WORLD

*Learning How to Renew and
Protect Your Mind*

David E. Carr

New Wine Press

New Wine Ministries
PO Box 17
Chichester
West Sussex
United Kingdom
PO20 6YB

Scripture quotations are taken from the following versions of the Bible:

NKJV – The Holy Bible, New King James Version. Copyright © 1982 by
Thomas Nelson Inc.

NASB – New American Standard Bible. Copyright © 1960, 1962, 1963, 1968,
1971, 1972, 1973, 1975, 1977, 1995 by The Lockman Foundation.

NIV – The Holy Bible, New International Version. Copyright © 1973, 1978,
1984 by International Bible Society. Used by permission of Hodder and
Stoughton Limited.

KJV – The King James Version, Crown copyright.

ISBN 978 1 903725 42 9

Typeset by CRB Associates, Reepham, Norfolk
Cover design by CCD, www.ccdgroup.co.uk
Printed in Malta

CONTENTS

ACKNOWLEDGMENTS

As I started to teach and preach on the renewing of the mind, true spiritual thinking, and the need to deal with the damage of youth, a number of Christian leaders encouraged me to write a book on the topic – none more so than Richard Taylor, my deputy in the ministry and a spiritual son. By applying the principles himself, the transformation in Richard's own life since he was converted in a prison in Swansea is amazing. He kept nagging me until I started writing!

Great thanks goes to Tim Pettingale, Director of New Wine Press, who has taken my chaotic thoughts and words and crafted them into chapters – thank you.

Thank you Yvonne East, Barbara Carstairs and Sarah Hickey for typing the manuscript from my handwritten notes – not many people can understand Brummiese!

Thank you to Melvyn Carman, my ministry colleague when I travel, for proof reading this book and for booking yourself in to see a psychiatrist!

Thank you Molly for being a great wife – you could have written this book about me! Ashley, Melanie, Lucy – sadly I never understood fully the role of a father until you had passed childhood, yet I am privileged that you still love me.

Thank you to Renewal – you are a great church – and to all my spiritual children and grandchildren – I love you.

INTRODUCTION

As I was sitting in my church office one day, dealing with myriad activities as usual: conferences to organise, sermons to write ... I was interrupted by the phone ringing. It was my PA. She had just received a call to inform us that a young man had been found hanging in his home. It was the second phone call of its kind I had received that day. Earlier that morning a divorced man living on his own had taken his own life.

The shock and grief gripped me. The young man, a well educated boy, had been suffering from schizophrenia and had recently made contact with the church. The divorced man had just finished the Alpha Course and was beginning to make friends. Yet, we got to them too late.

That day I decided that, in so far as I was able, I could not let this happen again. We immediately started a fund to raise money for the purchase of a clinic to help these tormented people.

During thirty-three years as a pastor it has always been my conviction that there is much more to the Christian gospel than the appeal to "Give your heart to Jesus."

Following their initial commitments to Christ, many believers continue to live with negative thinking, are easily offended, and find it difficult to forgive others. Why is this? I believe it is because *the mind* needs to be given much more attention. It is my hope that through this book many will find a new freedom as they begin to renew their minds and bring their thoughts into line with God's, enjoying the surpassing peace that process affords.

David Carr
July 2005

CHAPTER 1

FOR UNTO US
A CHILD IS
BORN

The book of Proverbs contains thirty-one chapters of distilled wisdom. My father used to say to me, "Son, read one every day of the month and you won't go wrong." Psychologists would concur with that prognosis, because it has long been proven that what a child comes to believe during his/her formative years (generally the first seven), leaves a lifetime's impression. During those early years deep furrows are carved in the mind as the child develops psychologically, emotionally and spiritually. Values, either positive or negative, are instilled. The influences that are brought to bear on the child will shape the man/woman they will become in the future. It is my belief that many of the mental problems that people suffer later in life find their root in dysfunctional childhood development. For that reason I want to explore in this opening chapter both the negative and positive effects of childhood "training". If we practise godly and loving discipline, we will save our kids from a host of problems later in life. In later chapters we will look more closely at the mental problems that can affect adults and we will learn how to fully submit our minds to Christ.

Honour and Discipline

The values that many of my generation held (the mid-1940s to early fifties) no longer seem to be cherished today. The exhortation of the apostle Paul in his letter to the Ephesians is a lost voice in modern society:

> *"Children, obey your parents in the Lord, for this is right. 'Honour your father and mother (which is the first command-ment with a promise), so that it may be well with you, and that you may live long on the earth.' Fathers, do not provoke your children to anger, but bring them up in the discipline and instruction of the Lord."*
>
> (Ephesians 6:1–4 NASB)

I would like to unpack these words of Paul further, because I believe they are so important for us to understand today. Many modern parents have abandoned good discipline for their children, and I believe that this is one of the root causes of so many "mental" problems that plague individuals in adulthood.

Firstly, Paul commands children to obey their parents in the Lord. His assumption is that this is entirely normal and right. Secondly, he says, *"Honour your father and mother."* This command has a double promise attached to it:

1. That it may be *well* with you.
2. That you may live long on the earth.

Thirdly, there is an instruction to fathers: "Don't provoke your children to anger, but discipline or *train* them." Elsewhere in the Bible we read the confirmation,

> *"**Anxiety** in the heart of man causes depression,*
> *But a **good word** makes it glad."*
> (PROVERBS 12:25 NKJV, emphasis added)

Here we see a link between anxiety leading to depression and a "good word" leading to gladness. A "good word" here can be interpreted as being corrective; a word of guidance. Shortly after in Proverbs we read,

> *"He who spares his rod hates his son,*
> *But he who loves him disciplines him promptly."*
> (PROVERBS 13:24 NKJV)

The discipline of children is a highly emotive issue for many, but according to Scripture, any parent that neglects loving discipline early in a child's life has little true love for him/her and shows a total disdain for the child's future ability to exercise self-discipline in times of emotional trial. The Bible tells us that if a father does not instruct his child then he/she will become reckless and unable to follow wisdom:

> *"A wise son heeds his father's instruction,*
> *But a scoffer does not listen to rebuke."*
>
> (PROVERBS 13:1 NKJV)

Years after this warning was written, the apostle Paul, giving an illustration of God's father heart, asked the question, "Is there a father who would not correct the child he loves?" Sadly, the answer today would be "Yes, plenty!"

It appears that, whilst the twenty-first century claims the amount of children being assessed with Attention Deficit Syndrome (ADS) is increasing, this condition is not a recent discovery. It dates back to the mid eighteen hundreds when it was called "fidgeting disease". The question may be asked, does this increase in diagnosis coincide with a change in the style of parental discipline and training patterns? I believe it does.

As a child, any of my behavioural violations at school or home met with instant correction, though not necessarily physical punishment. My father never hit me throughout my life. Loss of privileges and detention were the main methods of correction, though at school there was controlled corporal punishment. If you were caught doing something wrong at school and punished, you would never, ever go home and tell your parents! You would have to have been a masochist to do so! The majority of parents in those days would say, "You must have done something wrong or you wouldn't have been punished!" And then you would get a second round of discipline!

How things have changed today. I serve as Chairman of the Governor's Discipline Board for a fine school in Solihull. Many of the parents' attitudes have changed dramatically. We meet in the context of their children having poor disciplinary records, to see how things might be improved. These are a sample of the kind of responses parents will give when challenged about their child's behaviour:

- "The teachers are picking on him."
- "The Head wants her out of the school."
- "They are lying."
- "I know my child is no angel but ... "

One can only conclude that for most children the "training" that the Bible speaks of has disappeared. Or has it?

Positive or Negative Training?

The reality is that training is always taking place. Whether we are conscious of it or not, our children are constantly being trained by us, be it structured or unstructured, positive or negative. By subjecting a child to a life with no safe boundaries or accountability, breaking promises to them, living an undisciplined lifestyle, making threats, using bad language, being aggressive etc., you are training that child for a life of confusion and rejection. This undefined programme of negative input will affect them subliminally, at its most subtle level, or be plainly destructive at its most blatant. Any negative influences, if not dealt with, will embed themselves in the malleable subconscious of a child. Physical, mental, emotional or sexual violations will leave an indelible scar.

The emotional and moral training of a child will take place one way or another. Those first seven years of life will lay foundations deep in the mind with lifelong characteristics being established. From the womb to the age of seven, more is assimilated than in any other period of a person's life: parental and human bonding, vision, sound, recognition, sitting, crawling, walking, talking, basic friendships, literacy, numeracy, language, and the foundation of self-esteem. It is also a time when children learn basic life disciplines such as eating, sleeping, toilet training and elementary social skills. My wife Molly often comments when we are eating out at a restaurant, how few children have any table manners or even know how to eat with a knife and fork!

Many of our reactions to situations are based on assumptions gleaned from previous experience. What we have been taught, good or bad, will automatically form our opinions, not based on the facts but on our emotional experience of what we assume are the facts. Few stop and ask for clarification and assumption is the father of many wrong decisions. It is often negative childhood experiences that will cause people to react unreasonably in what most would view as an innocent situation. Experiences that robbed them of their innocence as a child will prevent them from reaching maturity and set them back emotionally.

Numerous world movements seeking to bring about a

"reformation" have understood the importance of fashioning the minds of the young. Adolph Hitler with his youth
movement could rightly be described as having established
a military mind control organisation. It was the youth of
China who eventually heralded in the cultural revolution,
showing that even influences outside of the family can
change the direction of an impressionable mind. Even
religious groups have worked on this basis. It was the Jesuits,
taking their lead from Ecclesiastes, that made the well
known statement, "Give me the child and I will give you
the man."

Your childhood experiences stay with you throughout
your life. At the time of writing I have just celebrated my
sixtieth birthday, yet I can still remember the pledges I
swore as a cub scout at the age of seven, and as a member of
the Boys Brigade at eleven!

GOOD TRAINING HELPS OVERCOME LIFE'S PROBLEMS

Solomon in the book of Ecclesiastes reflects on the training
of children.

"Remember now your Creator in the days of your youth,
Before the difficult days come,
And the years draw near when you say,
'I have no pleasure in them.'"

(ECCLESIASTES 12:1 NKJV)

The condition of a child's mind and soul when they are
young can provide a strong foundation from which they can

cope with the pressures of life that will inevitably come. By introducing faith in Christ into the training of a child, you can give them a confidence and a strength that will help them overcome the unseen tribulations of later life.

Life's problems have never really changed throughout history, because history is full of people just like you and me. The scenery may differ, but the human heart remains the same. Solomon predicted that troubles would come as surely as night follows day, we just have different names for them now: redundancy, loneliness, ill health, phobias, or simply the experience of growing older. What is Solomon's answer to these future fears? Allow children to be instructed in the ways of God and a lot of heartache will be avoided.

In modern society this may be easier said than done. The importance of setting aside time to train and discipline children, instilling values and helping them to develop constructive habits, has been marginalised. How? Firstly, many parents have never had the opportunity to learn godly discipline themselves – so disciplining their children doesn't come easily. Secondly, it is more common now for both parents to be working and for the extended family to be more widely scattered. Children are receiving much of their training from TV, DVDs, and their peers, instead of their parents.

Children need constructive discipline to help shape their personality. I meet people who invest considerably more time in training their dogs how to "stay" and "fetch" than their children to be respectful and to value people. As I listen to many young people who manifest little sense of respect or concept of social values, it seems to me that it's their parents who need the "rod of correction", not the children! A lack of meaningful monitoring of their child's life is woefully evident in quotes such as, "They won't tell me where they are going ... what can you do? ... they grow up so quickly ... they won't listen to me any more ... "

Proverbs 22:6 says,

"Train up a child in the way he should go,
And when he is old he will not depart from it."

(NKJV)

That demands time, determination and love. Remember the warning given to potential dog owners? "A dog is for life, not just for Christmas." Well, the same is true of children!

My granddaughter Poppy is three months old. My son-in-law Nathan has started as I hope he means to continue. He reads to her every night; takes her shopping; feeds her; baths and changes her; takes her to the park to see the ducks. She is being integrated into the world and Nathan is changing his behaviour in order to accommodate her into the family. Poppy comes with them to church on Sunday mornings and during the week my daughter Lucy brings Poppy into the church office to see Granddad. What are they doing? What nobody taught me to do as a young pastor with children. They are training Poppy, laying foundations for her to build her dreams, without being encumbered by other less important issues.

We have a number of spiritual grandchildren. We always seek to love them and encourage them. We are trying to show them by our actions that we believe they are valuable, because it is a fundamental lack of self-worth that sows the seed for future emotional trauma.

HAPPY CHILDHOOD?

Our early years are the most precious and impressionable of our whole life. To have a childhood full of happy, positive memories, does not necessarily guarantee emotional stability in later life, but will limit future problems and diffuse some of the emotional time bombs that others live with.

What makes a child happy? Often we misinterpret "happiness" by showering our children with an abundance of material things gained without merit, thinking this will make them happy and fulfilled, but often such gifts are motivated by guilt and are poor replacements for spending time together.

If however, we lay foundations which have value and merit at their core, our children will grow up to love us more than words can say; much more than if we are only distant gift-givers who never get deeply and personally involved in their lives. I have seen many families who have little in the way of material things to give their kids, yet their love and commitment to one another is amazing.

My Son Ashley is different from me in so many ways. I am larger than life; he's quiet and willing to take a back seat. Ashley has a degree in Fine Art and we have many heated discussions on the merits of Cubism! He is a man of gentleness and integrity, slow to push himself forward. This is a frustration to me, as I know he is an excellent photographer and worthy of many commissions.

My daughter Melanie is so different. She likes to confront, be in your face, and is the life and the soul of the party, just like Dad. Lucy, my youngest daughter is like her brother, with a little bit of me!

One Father's Day I received a card from Ashley that simply said, "To say that we are the same would not be true. Yet all your values are my values too."

Your children can and must have their own personalities, yet it is so important they are taught good values. It is that which dwells in the most intimate part of our consciousness that determines who we are and what our perceptions are. Our values prejudge so many situations we find ourselves in during life.

THE FIVE SENSES

God created us with five senses through which we perceive and understand the world: smell, taste, sight, hearing and touch. The stimulation of the senses plays an important part in fashioning childhood development, educationally, emotionally and physically. The senses also play an important part in a child's spiritual experience.

Smell
My father worked at Cadbury's as a leather worker, manufacturing the great conveyer belts that delivered the chocolate. For me, two smells immediately identified "Dad" – chocolate and leather. The smell of chocolate would cling to his clothes when he returned from work, and I remember the smell of leather when he repaired our shoes and made us cases for school in his workshop at home. Both of

these smells still fondly remind me of him twenty years after his death.

Taste

Taste plays a big part in most people's memories. As a kid I found the taste of cabbage absolutely repulsive! But I was born at a time in history when you did not leave the dinner table until you had eaten all your food. At that time food was still rationed. For some strange reason that bad experience stayed with me until I had my tonsils out at twenty-one. After that I loved all my greens. It must have been psychological!

Sight

What we see as a child can leave a lasting impression for good or evil. My mother showed me some water as a child and told me that if I went near it I would either die or develop pneumonia. As a result I developed a deep phobia of water and it was not until I was forty-eight that Andy Earles, a spiritual son, helped me to confront my deepest fear and learn to swim. I thank God for Andy. My mother had transferred her own fear onto her three sons.

Sight is so powerful. The following story is true and traumatic:

A family of refugees from the war in Croatia came into our church and became Christians. They came from a Muslim village with their two children – a boy and a girl. The little boy would have been six or seven when he arrived in England in the back of a truck.

A child psychologist who was assessing the emotional effect on the children of leaving their home and entering the UK, asked the boy to draw what he saw in his mind when he thought about his home and the village he came from. He drew a picture that showed matchstick men with wavy lines coming from them. When asked what that represented the boy said, "Those are the burning dead bodies in the street by my house." This image of death had been forged deep in the memory of this little boy. If not dealt with it would have life-long consequences on his emotional wellbeing. Most fears and phobias start in child-hood and manifest in many different ways. In later life a person often cannot even recall the original trauma that triggered their fears.

This little boy and his sister badly missed their granddad back in Croatia. In times of trouble they had often cuddled up to him and fallen asleep on his chest, for once feeling safe from the dangers outside. One Sunday morning after the service I was greeting this family when the two children started to cry for their granddad. I decided immediately that Molly and I would become surrogate grandparents to these two frightened children.

Once we took them to a theme park and they began to cry as they watched Molly pay the £50 entrance fee. "Molly," they cried, "we are not worth that amount of money." As the days turned into weeks however, their confidence grew. I told them that they needn't be afraid of anything because Jesus had special angels whose job it was to watch over them. In Psalm 23 the Bible says that goodness and mercy will follow us all the days of our life. I told them, "Remember, goodness and mercy are like 'bodyguard angels' protecting us from behind."

One year later the same child psychologist conducted a

further assessment of the children as part of their appeal to remain in the UK. Again he asked the boy to draw a picture – this time relating to his life in Solihull. The boy drew three angels. The psychologist asked why he had drawn them and what it meant. The boy replied, "I am now a Christian and my English granddad told me that I have angels looking after me. The two big ones who follow me are called 'goodness' and 'mercy' and they will stay with me all of my life, so I am not frightened any more."

The fear of death had been replaced by the promise of life and protection. A negative can only be replaced by the promise of a positive, but the positive must be able to be grasped. The promise of safety to two little children started by reaching out with the arms of love and our desire to act to remove that fear.

Hearing

The words we hear spoken over us as kids resonate for years to come. Negative words spoken in anger or frustration can still be heard decades on in the minds of people who are now adults and can limit us and hold us back. Children do not have the ability or maturity to access situations and to make allowances for the shortfalls or frailty of adults. What they hear they believe. If they hear negative things spoken about them, whether it's from their parents, school friends or even the media, those things will lay a faulty foundation for their life. Conversely, positive words and loving affirmation will show their benefits years after the conversation has taken place.

The Bible teaches us that hearing is essential for the Christian life. Waiting on and listening to God is a vital discipline to learn that will result in steady spiritual growth and wellbeing. Jesus said, "If any man hears My voice ... " God is constantly speaking to us, but we must learn to listen.

Touch

Touch is such a powerful tool in the development of a child, it is a tragedy that its use has been so weakened by emotional, physical and sexual abuse. Out of a desire to protect children from harm, political correctness is leaving children devoid of physical contact. There is much less hugging and embracing these days and a disdain for smacking is creating a generation who are incapable of discerning the touch of love and correction.

These days a teacher cannot even place their hand on a pupil's shoulder (either expressing affirmation or correction) without the action being misinterpreted by someone. Yet, in the midst of such a touch-less society violence among young people or against the elderly is escalating. Could it be because appropriate touch is no longer part of children's emotional development?

Jesus knew the power of touch. He touched a leper and in the process put Himself adrift of the "legal" requirements of the church for ceremonial purity. He held the hand of a dead child and raised her to life.

The story is told of a married man who found that his wife was becoming increasingly depressed. He was unable to spend much time with her and as the illness grew worse he booked for her to see a consultant psychiatrist. Just ten minutes into the interview the elderly doctor stood up from his desk, walked over to the woman, asked her to stand up and put his arms around her. She wept and wept. After the interview was over the doctor said to the husband, "I have found the remedy. Your wife needs a hug every day." The husband said, "That's fine doctor, but with work and golf I can only bring her Monday's and Thursdays." That's not far from the truth is it?

Some time ago we had the first Sunday meeting at one of our new church plants. We held the meeting in the local town hall, fifteen miles away from the central church. It was 6.00pm and the service was about to begin. As I looked from the steps of the town hall towards the nearby shopping mall I saw an old lady who was obviously looking around to find the church. I walked over to her and asked if I could help. She said she was looking for the new church and so I said I would walk her to the meeting. As we walked along, sadness was engraved on her face. I held her hand and led her up the steps. As we came to the door she started to cry and asked me who I was. I told her I was the Senior Pastor. She thanked me and told me that since her husband died some years ago, no one had ever held her hand. This simple act released a deep sense of loss that had been trapped inside, unable to find expression.

Our family is a kissing family. My father always liked to kiss us and tell us he loved us before any of us left the home. Consequently, I have always found it easy to kiss people. I do this when I pray for the sick. I find myself kissing young and old, men and women, with devastating effect! I've had grown men weep and say, "I always wanted my dad to do that to me. Thank you." My three children Ashley, Melanie and Lucy would never say goodbye without a kiss and "I love you."

These are all simple actions – connecting with people through the five senses – but they make such a difference. For children especially, creating positive experiences through smell, taste, sight, hearing and touch will help them to develop as whole individuals who will not feel isolated or afraid in later life.

✔ HEALTH CHECKLIST

Points covered in this chapter:

▶ Experiences during the formative years of a person's life leave a lifetime's impression.

▶ Early influences, either positive or negative, shape the person you become in adulthood.

▶ Much modern parenting is neglecting godly, loving discipline and this is a major cause of an unstable mind.

▶ We are constantly training our children whether we realise it or not. Positive training will avert a host of problems in later life.

▶ The five senses through which we perceive and connect with the world are vital to the foundation of a sound mind.

CHAPTER 2

EVERYONE HAS PSYCHOLOGICAL PROBLEMS!

"Therefore I say to you, do not worry about your life, what you will eat or what you will drink; nor about your body, what you will put on. Is not life more than food and the body more than clothing? Look at the birds of the air, for they neither sow nor reap nor gather into barns; yet your heavenly Father feeds them. Are you not of more value than they? Which of you by worrying can add one cubit to his stature?

"So why do you worry about clothing? Consider the lilies of the field, how they grow: they neither toil nor spin; and yet I say

to you that even Solomon in all his glory was not arrayed like one of these. Now if God so clothes the grass of the field, which today is, and tomorrow is thrown into the oven, will He not much more clothe you, O you of little faith?

"Therefore do not worry, saying, 'What shall we eat?' or 'What shall we drink?' or 'What shall we wear?' For after all these things the Gentiles seek. For your heavenly Father knows that you need all these things. But seek first the kingdom of God and His righteousness, and all these things shall be added to you. Therefore do not worry about tomorrow, for tomorrow will worry about its own things. Sufficient for the day is its own trouble."

(MATTHEW 6:25–34 NKJV)

I have been challenged for many years about the problem of mental illness and how each one of us is affected by it to one degree or another. We have a tendency to categorise only the most *extreme* cases as "mental illness", but the fact is, every person reading this book has some form of psychological defect! Each of us must have, as I will explain more fully later, because sin has brought that about.

Most of us live in denial. We believe it's always the next person who has the problem and that our mental processes are in good working order. This of course neatly sums up the human condition: we always think that *we* are the ones who are in control. We think we are misunderstood by others, yet *we* never misunderstand them. We think we always hear clearly what is being said to us, yet so often we misinterpret things or fail to grasp what was *really* being communicated.

I have proven this myself many times in the past. One

thing I regularly do in leadership seminars is to ask people to write down the first thing that comes into their mind upon hearing a simple statement. I have found that people's diverse cultural background and upbringing will cause them to automatically respond in a certain way to a given statement. Typically I ask people to write what they feel should follow on from the words: "Mary had a little lamb ... "

All those who have a British cultural background will tend to write down, " ... whose fleece was white as snow." But if I was speaking to a group of leaders in Bulgaria, for instance, they would not have a clue what the statement meant, because it is an English nursery rhyme, and would no doubt respond very differently. If I was speaking at a Catholic seminary, they might respond, " ... His name was Jesus." Perhaps if I put this statement before a seasoned farmer, he would respond, "No big deal – all my sheep have lambs, what's so special about Mary?"!

The point is, we tend to view and understand the world through the filter of our personal background, culture, education and life experience. These peculiarities, unique to us, dictate how we will respond to things. In the case of my simple statement, "Mary had a little lamb ... " our background governs what immediately springs to mind and what we will say next.

Essentially, this happens every time a preacher stands in front of a congregation. It would be true to say that none of my church members actually "hear" the sermons that I preach! Rather they interpret them to the best of their ability, because they don't actually *know* what was in my mind when I wrote the sermon and why God gave me that message; they have no way of gauging the impact that it made on me when I received it from the Lord. The extent to which people really grasp the message is proportionate to my ability to deliver it – but ultimately no one will "get" the message I originally "got".

Remember the old war-time joke about communication? A messenger was sent out from the front line battle with the message: "Going to advance ... send reinforcements!" By the time he reached the head quarters the message he actually delivered was, "Going to a dance ... send three and fourpence"!

So, communication between individuals is problematic enough, but why do I believe that each of us has "mental problems"? Because Jesus highlighted it early on in His ministry as we will see.

Do Not Worry

In Matthew chapter 6 Jesus confronts an issue which has been around for many centuries. Worry, stress, pressure, and mental illness are not products of a twenty-first century lifestyle – they have been with humanity ever since the fall. We read in the Old Testament that many kings became demented. One was so disturbed he acted like an animal and ate grass! King Saul used to become mentally unstable and David had to come and play music to him to sooth and calm him. As a result, one of Jesus' key instructions to all believers was, "Do not worry".

Both Matthew and Luke pick up on Jesus' statement about not worrying. But Luke's eye for detail means that he also captures a beautiful, comforting phrase that Jesus adds to His main comments: *"Fear not, little flock"* (Luke 12:32 KJV). What a wonderful expression! It perfectly captures the image of the Shepherd caring for His sheep. Jesus saw that in His time, and in the future, mental, emotional and psychological illnesses would be rife, and yet He says to believers, *"Fear not, little flock."* Jesus is dealing with the very important subject of mental wholeness.

In my experience, it is easier for somebody to come to faith and be born again in the Spirit than it is to change the way they think. A pastor spends more of his time trying to persuade people out of their old mindset than he does getting them into the kingdom. Heaven forbid, if you were to backslide and leave your church, the chances are it would not be because of your *spirit*, but because of your *mind* – because of what you believe people think about you, or what you think of them.

MENTAL HEALTH IN GRIDLOCK

Many people's view of *mental health* is still gridlocked in the middle ages. It is one of the medical sciences that has progressed very little over the centuries. We now think of heart transplants as quite normal. Heart bypasses are routine, ten a penny. In many ways bypasses are no more difficult for a doctor to undertake than removing your appendix. Thousands take place every year. We have become blasé about such operations, even though they require major surgery. Surgery that used to take months of rehabilitation has now reached a level of sophistication in its technique that means recovery times are dramatically shorter.

A while back I had some heart trouble and had to go into hospital for some tests. They put a tiny isotope in my veins so that it could circulate around my body and glow, enabling the doctors to detect any blockages. They said this procedure was, "completely safe". I wanted to know why, if it was so safe, the radiologist was wearing a rubber suit and what looked like a bee-keeper's helmet, plus there was a big sign saying "Danger Radioactive"!

The Church's view of mental health is perhaps worse than that of the average person on the street. Christians will often attribute any signs of mental disorder to the demonic – a view that has not really changed much since the middle ages, we just express it in different terms. Anyone who manifests any form of mental illness that produces a change of character *must* be demonised, we think. Yet people don't attribute a broken leg, sinusitis or coronary thrombosis to the demonic, do they? It is time for the Church to operate with godly wisdom and discernment to confront the problem of mental illness.

TYPES OF MENTAL DISORDERS

Genetic

Mental disorders can fall into many categories, including genetic. Families can be susceptible to mental conditions just as they are to other illnesses such as heart disease or cancer. Therefore some people are born mentally and psychologically damaged because of the DNA makeup of their parents. Some might call that a curse? It is a curse in one sense, but it may not be a demonic curse – just a limitation. We do after all, live in a fallen world! There are some families in which, for instance, all the male members have died before reaching the age of sixty. Such things are not necessarily down to the devil – they can be genetic weaknesses in the family line. However, I don't believe that any person has to accept and tolerate whatever they have inherited. The Lord can set any person free.

One of the first questions I would ask of a person with a mental disorder is, "Is there anyone in your family with similar problems?" If they say, Yes, my uncle, my brother etc., then clearly it's genetic unless they've been into witchcraft. You can't say it's demonic if the people have lived a better life than you!

Demonic

Of course, there are those whose problems genuinely do stem from demonic affliction and these require special handling. On one occasion I was ministering at a church in Wales when I came across a girl who worked as a lap dancer. She had been in hospital after suffering an attack where somebody had spiked her drink and tried to rape her. She had actually heard me preach once when she was a young girl, and as she was lying in hospital, God spoke to her and told her to go to this specific church where she would find me. She had no idea whether I would really be there or not, but she went anyway and there I was. As soon as she walked in the building I felt prompted to begin speaking in tongues and at that moment she began manifesting and was thrown all over the room. She was actually crawling all over the seats like a snake and all hell broke loose for almost an hour until she was finally delivered.

As spiritual beings our minds, if not fully surrendered to Christ, can be vulnerable to attack. Mark chapter 5 and Luke chapter 8 tell the story of "Legion" a demon possessed man whose life was dominated by these fallen spirits. His desire to inflict self-harm is now known to be a classic sign of psychological problems. Clearly he was mentally deranged, but the voices in his head could not be attributed to schizophrenia, they were real! The very presence of Jesus threw him into mental and spiritual torment. The result of Jesus' intervention was that he was set free spiritually, physically and mentally. After deliverance we read that he was *". . . sitting and clothed and in his right mind"* (Mark 5:15 NKJV). His whole person – spirit, soul and body – had been brought into harmony through Christ.

Hormonal

Whilst there are isolated cases such as the one above, much mental illness is not demonic, but the result of a decaying human mind in a decaying world. Another type of mental illness is the result of hormonal imbalances. When the interaction of chemicals in the human body gets out of sync, the area most affected tends to be the brain – the control centre of everything we are. When the hormones are out of balance then the mind becomes disturbed and attacked causing unnatural manifestations.

Hormonal imbalances can affect men and women, yet the problem is considerably higher among women. This can in some cases can be compounded by the menstrual cycle, or later the menopause.

Lifestyle

Your lifestyle too can affect your mental health in a positive or negative way. You can work too hard and suffer a mental breakdown; you can also work too little and have a breakdown. The pace of life that people are living at today can easily lead to mental and emotional burnout. With unparalleled levels of stress and pressure in both work and family life, there is a real need for us to change our lifestyles and to discharge much of that pressure into relaxing pastimes such as music, sport, art or literature etc.

Mental illness can be brought on as a result of a lifestyle of substance abuse – using either drugs or alcohol. In the next chapter I will touch on the reason I believe people are drawn to drugs and alcohol particularly, but for now, let's look at some of the facts.

Drugs

Even prescribed drugs given with good intentions in mind can lead into addiction. One Canadian woman fell into addiction after being prescribed a cocktail of tranquilisers, sleeping pills and anti-depressants following the death of her four-year-old son with a brain tumour. For twenty years she faced "addiction by prescription" which later became the title of the book telling her story.[1]

Certain drugs can trigger mental health problems, particularly in young people and those who have any history of mental illness. When any substance invades the complexity of the brain, adverse side effects will be the result. In the UK cannabis was recently downgraded to a class C drug. To many it is no more harmful than tobacco, yet most doctors agree that persistent use of this drug can lead to schizophrenia.

Alcohol

Alcohol abuse can induce a psychosis similar to schizophrenia. One study on women with alcohol problems found that younger women who were alcoholics were twice as likely to attempt suicide than older women, and that 88% of alcoholic women tried to commit suicide compared to 40% of non-alcoholic women.[2]

Two of my leadership team have come from a history of drug addiction after being born again and receiving rehabilitation from Victory Outreach and Teen Challenge. Both would maintain that alcohol is one of the two hardest addictions to break (nicotine being the other). Fewer alcoholics who have been through rehabilitation programmes manage to stay clean than those who have used hardcore drugs such as heroin or cocaine.

Personal image

The personal image obsessed society that we live in has created an increasing number of lifestyle illnesses as people, mainly women, strive to achieve what they perceive as physical perfection:

- *Anorexia*: a condition where an individual refuses to maintain a minimum normal body weight due to the false perception that they are overweight.

- *Bulimia*: a pattern of binge eating followed by purging. Individuals feel guilty and angry after binging on food. 90% of bulimics then engage in self-induced vomiting. They may also try to lose weight using inappropriate methods such as the misuse of laxatives, diuretics, fasting, enemas etc. A bulimic's body weight can vary by up to 10lbs per day.

Apart from such obvious abuses of the body and their associated mental problems, it is also possible to have an accident that results in mental illness, for example, a cranial impact that causes brain damage, perhaps through a car crash or a bad fall.

Behavioural disorders

Many people today are being diagnosed with behavioural conditions that originate from a disturbed mind. Such behavioural conditions include afflictions such as Tourette's Syndrome, Attention Deficit Hyperactivity Disorder, Obsessive Compulsive Disorder (OCD) and many others.

On one occasion, a leader visited our church with his wife. She had suffered for thirty-seven years with OCD. She would never stay in a place overnight for fear of germs and disease and she had established a pattern of washing herself many times a day. That day I was preaching on the topic of "The return of glory to the Christian church" and during the sermon the Holy Spirit spoke to this lady and said, "Will you repent of this obsession?" The cry of her heart in response was, "But it's not my fault!". But the Spirit spoke and asked her again and this time she said, "Yes, Lord." Immediately she was set free and God made her whole.

Some time later I received a letter from her very thankful husband who was jubilant about the fact that God had healed his wife. I put the letter down and asked the Lord, "Why did this lady need to repent of her condition? She was, after all, affected by it almost from birth." The answer came to me swiftly and clearly: "Because to repent means to change the direction of your thinking." Of course, to repent means to turn around completely and go the opposite way. She was not so much repenting of a sin she had committed, but was cooperating with the Holy Spirit to change the well-worn patterns of thought that had entrapped her for so long. As her mind was renewed by the Spirit, she could now live with the consequences of her healing and rise above the temptation to regress back into her mental disorder.

OCD is often referred to as "Doubting Disease". As with many similar syndromes, they can rob a person of many hours each day as they engage in their particular compulsion, and this also brings stress and distress on their wider family. Lesley E. Packer, PhD, has defined such obsessive compulsions as,

> "... repetitive behaviour or mental acts that the person feels driven to perform in response to an obsession or according to rules that must be applied rigidly. These behaviours or mental acts are usually aimed at preventing or reducing stress or preventing some dreaded event or situation. Importantly the compulsive behaviours are not usually connected to the worrying thought. For example a child may be plagued with an obsessive worry that if they don't turn the light switch on and off perfectly exactly 32 times he will come home to find his dog slashed and mutilated. Children are not fully aware that others don't have these obsessive behaviour patterns and by the time they do most times they will 'cover up' these compulsions."

In researching these things I have realised how many of us have at least a mild form of this disorder. When travelling abroad over the years, I would always, before leaving the house, take my travel documents out of my briefcase and check them at least three times. Have you ever checked that you have locked the windows and doors in your house two or three times, just to convince yourself that you definitely did it? It's a doubt syndrome: "Did I do it?" Another manifestation of this same condition is when people have to have objects lined up in a particular way, or arranged "just right", otherwise they feel discomfort or, in extreme cases, the onset of deep fear. Most of us have concerns and doubts over diverse issues, but to those with compulsion disorders it is the dominant factor of their life.

THE NEED FOR DISCERNMENT

Because our lives are so interwoven between mind, body and spirit it is often difficult to discern whether an illness is spiritually-based or physiologically-based. That's why the gift of discernment is so essential if you are dealing with mentally ill people and are praying for their healing.

Once when I was speaking about this topic at a conference, two dear ladies approached me, both of whom had problems with mental illness. They told me that their church had spent every week for a year trying to cast demons out of them. These women were utterly exhausted by this process; they were desperate. One of them told me that because her husband would not join in the "exorcism", the church leaders no longer thought he was saved – because "all Christians should be able to cast demons out of people"! I put my arms around these women and said, "You just need a bit of tender loving care, the Word of God fed into you, and you need to keep your minds fixed on Jesus."

Another woman was thought to "have a demon" just because she had had four babies die on her. Surely that is enough to mentally distress any woman? Her church leaders were of the bizarre opinion that because she became deeply depressed during the birth, a demon must have entered her through the womb! Personally, I would like to get hold of some of these Christians and hold their heads under water for a long time! It makes me so angry! They are the sort of people who will end up getting church gatherings banned in Europe with their unbiblical ideas! It is so important when seeking to minister to individuals that we have the mind of Christ – that we listen carefully to what the Holy Spirit is saying and act accordingly.

Salvation and healing are unified in the word "wholeness". What I desire more than anything is to see people really made "whole". You will often find that even Christians who have been saved out of a life of addiction or obsession still carry some of those traits over into the kingdom of God. They may be disguised as radicalism, fervour, zeal and commitment, yet the underlying drive is an addictive or obsessive personality that has not been fully dealt with. I have seen such hidden problems manifest themselves various ways: reading vast amounts of Scripture, excessive times of fasting, prayer, even giving. In themselves they are all good biblical things to do! Yet taken to extremes because of guilt, hyperactivity or excessive frustration they only result in the person being driven and not led.

Jesus said, *"My sheep hear My voice, and I know them, and they follow Me"* (John 10:27 NKJV). Following is not merely passive, but it is relational and directional. As we follow Jesus we are choosing to place our confidence in Him and the direction He is setting for our life journey. It is interesting to see the philosophical difference between shepherding in Eastern and Western culture. In the East they lead their sheep, while in the West they drive them. What a lesson for the leaders of their flocks in the Western Church!

Having looked at the various different categories of mental or emotional illness, it naturally poses the question, "Should believers ever take medication to treat such illnesses, or just believe for God to heal them?" Many Christians would say no to medication, but I am not of that opinion. Over the last five years we have seen many wonderful healings in our church including a number of mental disorders – healings that not only needed medical confirmation, but received medical endorsement. At no time did we recommend ceasing medication. If a person has been healed then their medication will either cease having its effect or it will produce obvious side effects. Jesus told the man who He healed from leprosy to go and show himself to the priest (Matthew 8:1–4). The priest was the only person who was authorised to "sign him off" and allow him to return to normal life. We have a number of doctors in our church, as well as many nurses and pharmacists. Let them have the responsibility of declaring the sick healed. Until then, "keep taking the tablets"!

✔ HEALTH CHECKLIST

Points covered in this chapter:

▶ Everyone is affected by problems with their mind to one degree or another. No one is immune.

▶ Jesus highlighted the fact that worry, stress and mental anxiety would be a major problem for people down the ages.

▶ Many people's view of mental health is outdated and arcane. The views of the Church have at times been worse than those of people ''on the street''.

▶ Mental disorders fall into many categories and manifest themselves in a variety of ways. For this reason, spiritual discernment is vitally important when seeking to minister to others.

CHAPTER 3

GOD
AND THE
HUMAN MIND

The human mind and the un-regenerated spirit struggles
with the concept of God. I believe however, that the human
mind struggles much more with the concept of atheism
than it does with God, and I have seen this truth reflected in
the lives of sufferers of mental illness. The human mind is
constantly crying out to God. That's why so many people
who are hospitalised due to mental illness constantly talk
about God. In their state of utter confusion their spirit is
calling out to God, "Where are you? Help me!" So when

mentally ill people say, "God told me this or that", it is not necessarily demonic, but an outward manifestation of a confused mind calling to its Creator, "Get me out of this mess!"

Atheism is an alien concept to the human mind as God created it. It is not the natural starting point for man's thinking. God created man *in His image* and therefore the human mind is intended to reflect the thought patterns of God Himself. God made us and He made our minds to have a knowledge and understanding of Him. If God is not present in our life by His Spirit, then our minds will be disturbed and troubled by His absence. When a little child is separated from their parent they quickly become distressed and cry out, "Mummy ... Daddy!" Nobody else will do. Similarly, when a person becomes mentally ill they begin crying out, "I want my Creator!" Thank God that Jesus said, "Do not worry little flock" – He was letting us know that "Daddy" is here.

As soon as Adam sinned and fell, he could no longer enjoy the privilege of walking with God in the cool of the day. Instead of enjoying sweet fellowship with God and sharing his Father's thoughts, fear, concealment and self-justification began to invade the thought life of the human race. Those thoughts never existed until sin entered the world. Man's sanity was guaranteed as long as his mind was set and fixed on God. Adam had the mindset of Almighty God because He was created to think like God did and to speak things into being like God did. But sin brought confusion to his mind. Suddenly Adam was fearful and unsure of himself: "Why are you hiding?" God asked. "Because I'm frightened ...!"

Fear Inhabits the Space Where God's Presence is Absent

Fear came to occupy the place in Adam's mind where God had been shut out. That's why we can take comfort in the promise of the Bible that the perfect love of Jesus casts out all fear. Fear and God cannot inhabit the same place. Fear is the absence of God's presence and sin reflects the thoughts of a man whose mind is void of life and does not hear the voice of God.

One of the characteristics of schizophrenia is that sufferers will often "hear voices". They are not always demonic voices (though some are). It is a form of "overflow" of the person's subconscious thoughts. In essence the subconscious invades the conscious. The voices that a person will often hear in their head as they are dreaming, spill out into their present reality and they find it hard or impossible to tell the difference between fantasy and reality. The brain has lost its ability to distinguish between the conscious and the subconscious.

Hope lies in the words of Paul in the second chapter of 1 Corinthians when he teaches that it is possible for us, through Christ, to have our minds restored and "re-connected" to the thought patterns of the Creator, just like Adam before the fall: *"But we have the mind of Christ,"* he says (1 Corinthians 2:16 NKJV).

Man's spirit demands that the mind makes inquiries as to the possibilities of a Creator. How did we become Christians in the first place? Something happened in our spirit that prompted our mind to think about the question, "Who is God? Is He really there?" When the day came that we found ourselves in a meeting somewhere and the preacher preached a message, our mind received it and allowed the truth to go into our spirit. Our spirit then cried out, "Yes! This is what I've been looking for!" Our mind made a confession and our spirit came alive.

IS YOUR MIND FILLED WITH GOD?

In Corinthians Paul also spoke about being filled with God's mind (1 Corinthians 2:16), and warned of the consequences of not having our minds attuned to God. "If your mind is not stayed on Him," Paul says, then you are, "... *being filled with all unrighteousness, sexual immorality* [the thoughts are where sin begins], *wickedness, covetousness, maliciousness; full of envy, murder, strife, deceit, evil-mindedness ...* " (Romans 1:29 NKJV).

What a list! When the built-in conscience given to man by God Himself is deadened, the mind becomes independent and susceptible to confusion and depravity. With society constantly contradicting itself over its values and morality, the mind of man is left unstable and unsure of the basis of normality. 2 Peter 2:7 speaks about Lot who was "... *oppressed by the filthy conduct of the wicked*" (NKJV). Our minds, if subjected to constant pressure, will eventually absorb the flow of negative or subversive material. However, our minds are influenced by negative and positive signals only to the point of our heart's permissive attitude. If our heart refuses to accept something, then our mind will not receive it.

Paul also stresses that those people whose minds are not submitted to God become "whisperers" – in other words, "gossips". How amazing that according to Paul gossiping equals a psychological flaw, because we were not created to think like this! He goes on to list a number of other symptoms of the unregenerate mind. People become: "... *backbiters, haters of God, violent, proud, boasters, inventors of evil things, disobedient to parents* [also a "mental illness" Why? Because we were not created to have a dysfunctional relationship with our parents. It is a distortion of how our mind is intended to function], *undiscerning, untrustworthy, unloving, unforgiving, unmerciful*" (Romans 1:30–31 NKJV). All this describes a mind that has no influence of God in it! If our mind is not fixed on God, then Paul says it will be filled with all these other things.

You can understand then why the human mind is subject to such violation – having to contain all of that! That's why when we become a Christian it is so vital to deal with our thought life. We have to deal with our old way of thinking; our old attitudes. Paul says we can deal with it because we have the mind of Christ. Our mind can be renewed by His power.

A COUNTERFEIT EXPERIENCE OF THE SPIRIT

Drugs

I find it fascinating that people take drugs specifically so that their mind can be invaded by a chemical or plant extract that will bring an escapist sensation. People take drugs, either legally or illegally, that will help them to *escape* from their troubled mind for a while. Of course it is a false comfort and this "manufactured" relief is fleeting. The mind itself understands that the presence of a drug is an unnatural invasion and so it reacts with a warning in the form of side effects – some more dramatic than others. The mind says, I must react in some way, because this is not natural. This should not be happening!

Why do people seek after such sensations when we all know that they are temporal in effect and long term are highly damaging to our health? I believe it is man's attempt to recapture the rush of Holy Spirit flowing through his being. Escapism through substance abuse is a feeble attempt at counterfeiting the vivid realities of life in the awesome power of the Spirit.

People turn to drugs or alcohol because they recognise there is a massive void in their life – a void in their thinking and understanding that dates back to the fall of man; a void that did not exist when man's original state was still in tact and his mind was filled only with God. People are trying to simulate what only the Holy Spirit can give, which is the pure *peace of God*, the *pure purpose of God*, the *pure presence of God*. When the Holy Spirit comes powerfully upon a person, it causes a massive rush of adrenaline and well-being, and the world desperately wants to experience that.

If there is no rush of the Holy Spirit then alternatives must be sought out, usually resulting in extreme activities: binge drinking, sexual addictions, etc. Whatever it takes the void must be filled. The mind must be fed something that will titillate it and "keep up the ratings". The mind however, cannot be fooled. It still contains the receptive capabilities to pick up the Holy Spirit's call. Even in the heart of fallen man, the mind still knows how to send out the message, "Is there anybody out there?"

If God is the creator of true peace; if He is the giver of peace – a peace that cannot be found though human activity or philosophy – then the human mind will never know true completeness until it is established in Christ. But our society is given over to a debased or "reprobate" mind (that means a mind that is in absolute denial of the truth – the essence of mental illness).

Paul highlights this fact in Romans 1:28 when he says, *"And even as they did not like to retain God in their knowledge* [or in their mind], *God gave them over to a debased mind, to do those things which are not fitting"* (NKJV).

Drugs then, are a counterfeit manifestation of what only the Holy Spirit can truly give us. People take drugs because they need a lift, a kick, something to get them "up" or to bring them back down. Why? Because their lives are in crisis and they are often in denial about it. A person who knows true peace has no need of any "outside" stimuli.

Alcohol

Paul also warns in Ephesians 5:18, *"... do not get drunk with wine, for that is dissipation, but be filled with the Spirit"* (NASB).

Alcohol represents the foremost addiction in the world. It is harder to get addicts off alcohol than it is off cocaine, speed, or any other drug. Few hardened alcoholics ever get delivered. You can take a drug addict, keep him under close care for several months, ensure he stays clean and get him saved, and he may never touch drugs again. But if you help a man to get off alcohol, within a week he can be disappearing down to the off licence again.

Alcohol has become the foremost "substitute" to replace the feeling of wellbeing that only the Holy Spirit can give a person fully yielded to Christ. Even on my own church team there are three people who have had their lives decimated by partners who were constantly under the influence of alcohol. It can even affect believers who, through lack of good teaching in the church, do not show any proper constraint in drinking. The increase in "tippling" Christians is alarming! They do not see any danger, only their own liberty to indulge. Most think that any "weaker" brother and sisters, as the Bible puts it, who might be thrown by their behaviour, should just grow up!

In the last twenty years, according to government statistics, alcohol related deaths in the UK between the ages of fifteen and forty-four have tripled. These include deaths from health problems, accidents and even murders stemming from alcohol abuse. In the early 1980s only two percent of deaths among those age groups were attributed to alcohol. By 2001 this had risen to six percent.

Alcohol not only destroys the body, but places many in psychiatric care. Paul says it leads to "dissipation", that is, total confusion. It is a poor substitute. That's why Paul says not to drink wine to the extent that it leads you to have a *debased mind*. Rather than getting drunk, which will ultimately send you insane and ruin your kidneys, Paul says, "Why don't you get filled with the Holy Ghost?"

Whenever in Scripture we read this word "rather" it means there is *an alternative*! Rather than do that, do this! Paul says there is an alternative to alcoholism: being filled with the Spirit.

Paul says that if you are full of the Holy Spirit then you can live in the bliss of true peace without the need for outside stimuli. Each of us needs to have a place of escapism and to retreat into a world of our own sometimes. Paul says that in the Holy Spirit we can do that! You can retreat into His world! Be filled with the Spirit and know the peace of the secret place in God.

In my teens I once did six weeks nursing and worked on a ward full of alcoholics. These men hallucinated regularly because they had drunk so much. You had to actually laugh about the crazy things they would say, because otherwise it was too tragic to bear. I walked on to the ward one day and a guy grabbed me and said, "They've stolen the clock tower outside!" Deciding to humour him I looked out of the window and said, "Oh yeah, they have haven't they!" He was really agitated and he said to me, "Quick! Get the police!" I went out of the room for a minute and the sister said to me, "What's wrong?" I said, "He's hallucinating again." I walked back in and said, "It's OK, I've phoned the police," and he quickly responded, "What for?" "Because the clock tower's been stolen?" I ventured. "Don't be stupid," he said, "You can't steal a clock tower!" He had "come back" briefly. How can you live with a man like that? His mind had completely gone because of alcohol abuse.

Why is it that man tries to invent things that will replace the Holy Spirit? It is simply man's attempt to create a substitute for the presence of God. It is the world's way of trying to sooth the brain outside of the Holy Spirit – an impossible task.

I am praying for the finance to purchase a building which we will turn into a Christian clinic, the "Phileo Centre", to minister to those with mental and emotional illnesses. It will be staffed by fully trained and qualified people, and it will offer correct medication, dietary advice, prayer and study of the Scriptures, worship music therapy, and teach people how to build life disciplines. This Spirit-filled environment will bring the love of God and the discipline of light work and daily routines. Through it we want to enable people to return to be a part of their community. I believe this is a vision, not just a dream! The Lord has given us the command to go and preach the gospel of the Kingdom, heal the sick, bind up the broken hearted, and set the captives free.

In the following chapter we will look more closely at Jesus' command not to worry and learn how to shift our attention and desires away from our day to day concerns to focus on Jesus instead.

✔ HEALTH CHECKLIST

Points covered in this chapter:

▶ The fall of man heralded the fall of the human mind. It was at that point in human history that fear, concealment and self-justification first invaded man's thought life.

▶ Fear will occupy any space where God is not present. Hope is found in 1 Corinthians 2:16 where God promises to give us "the mind of Christ".

▶ A mind devoid of God will sink in a downward spiral of depravity. It is vital then, that we exercise control over our thought life and focus on Christ.

▶ People turn to alcohol and drugs to try to manufacture feelings of wellbeing that can only truly come as one is yielded to God and filled with the Holy Spirit.

CHAPTER 4

DON'T WORRY!

In our church we have a doctor trained in clinical psychology. Once, after I had been preaching on the subject of the mind, he came to me and said, "David, last week you preached for an hour on the subject of mental illness without any knowledge of your subject other than what God had given you to say. It was like you were preaching from a psychiatric textbook! You described schizophrenia in professional terms. I nudged my wife and said, 'If a psychiatrist was here today who wasn't a Christian, they would get saved.' Because they would realise that there was no way you could have known any of those things unless you had read a medical journal. God gave you complete insight into schizophrenia."

Now, why would God do that? Because today He is letting people know that the issue of the mind is on His agenda. God wants us to be whole people and a major key to our wholeness is peace of mind. One quarter of our population will be affected by mental instability. Though that seems an incredibly high percentage, it makes sense in the light of the fact that all have sinned and fallen short of God's glory. On that basis we are not operating with the patterns of thought that God created us to have. Instead our minds are corrupt and fallen, fractured and damaged.

Knowing this, Jesus spoke to His disciples, and all believers down the generations, and gave this command:

> *"Therefore I say to you, do not worry about your life ... "*
> (MATTHEW 6:25 NKJV, emphasis added)

Jesus puts things into perspective. He starts by saying, "Don't worry about your *life*." That covers every condition, every situation, every circumstance and event! He then goes on to give some examples of what He means.

Jesus tells us not to worry about what we will eat and drink, or about our bodies. So often people are preoccupied with questions like, Am I too fat ... too thin ... too tall ... too short ... Is my hair the wrong colour? What clothes should I wear? etc. But Jesus says, "Wait! Life is more than food and clothing!"

When Jesus spoke, He said things that were relevant to His day and had a present application, but His words were for the future too. Worrying is not a twenty-first century condition but one that has always existed. Jesus found it important enough to confront with His disciples and His words readily apply to our current climate. When Jesus spoke about not worrying about clothing, He spoke into a situation where there weren't many options. In those days it was either a plain cloak or a striped cloak – there wasn't a lot of choice! You didn't have Versace or any other designer labels to consider. But Jesus knew that it would be an issue for people in the future – very much so – and so His words resonate very clearly with us today.

God foresaw that a time would come when, if people weren't wearing the "right" clothing, they wouldn't even want to step outside their front door. The peer pressure that kids exert on each other today to be seen with the right clothes, trainers, mobile phone etc. is incredible. God saw ahead of time that boys would be bullied at school and refuse to go because their poor single parents can't afford £120 for the latest designer trainers that cost less than the cost of a burger to make in a sweat shop somewhere in the world.

Jesus knew that such matters would become a worry to people and so He instructs us, "Stop doing this! Stop worrying about such trivial matters!" It was no big deal in Jesus' day, but it is now. Jesus continues,

"Look at the birds of the air, for they neither sow nor reap nor gather into barns; yet your heavenly Father feeds them. Are you not of more value than they? Which of you by worrying can add one cubit to his stature? So why do you worry about clothing? Consider the lilies of the field, how they grow: they neither toil nor spin; and yet I say to you that even Solomon in all his glory was not arrayed like one of these. Now if God so clothes the grass of the field, which today is, and tomorrow is thrown into

the oven, will He not much more clothe you, O you of little faith?"

(MATTHEW 6:26–30 NKJV)

This passage of Scripture covers so many of people's phobias and fixations:

- *Life in general* – the stress of coping with the daily pressures or adversities we all face. Jesus says that worrying about it won't change anything!

- *Food* – the basic need for food and the overemphasis on eating too much or too little that people are so preoccupied with.

- *Self-image* – individuals in modern society are overwhelmed by the need to spend thousands of pounds on their image, whether it is by wearing the "right" clothing or by "reconstructing" themselves through surgery. Young and old alike are tormented by fashion and the fear of being ridiculed by others.

Think about the implications of what Jesus is saying here. He is saying that if we are full of worry then we are lacking in faith. The world may well worry about these things, Jesus is saying, but you who belong to the Father need not worry about anything, because He will certainly take care of all your needs. Yet, it's amazing how many Christians bring the world's values into the kingdom of God. We are told clearly that we don't need to worry, and yet we do.

Have you ever told your kids, "Eat all your dinner up because some children in the world are starving"? We've all said things like that at one time or another, but what is a statement like that really saying? In essence it's saying, "Don't worry about the little things because there are plenty of really big things to worry about", and yet God doesn't require us to worry on any level. It's just an example of how subtly the world's thinking impregnates believers' lives.

Jesus gives the antidote to all these problems:

"Seek first the kingdom of God and his righteousness, and all these things shall be added to you."

(MATTHEW 6:33 NIV)

In seeking, thinking about, and exploring the lifestyle of the kingdom of God we find a pattern of living and loving that brings true peace and tranquillity to our heart. Of all the qualities of the nature of Christ conferred upon us, righteousness is the key.

THE FACTS ABOUT WORRYING

According to the Mental Health Foundation, worrying is "a lasting preoccupation with past or future events". Worry and anxiety is something that effects every sector of society and is in no way exclusive to a particular group of vulnerable people. Worrying is a thought process that for many feels "out of control" as though they are unable to stem the flow of anxious thoughts. Worrying is characterised by phrases such as "But, what if …?" and "If only …". These phrases reveal the presence of limiting factors that are preventing a person from moving on from the past. Worry, anxiety, regret, pessimism, are all patterns of thought that immobilise our emotions, but we must not imprison our futures by negative thinking. "What if ... " thoughts are assumptions of future distress, but who knows what tomorrow will bring and who could control it even if they knew? No one – which is why worrying is so futile!

Worrying is merely the symptom of something deeper, but what is the root cause? When Jesus sought to confront the issue of worrying He was actually exposing an underlying lack of confidence in God and His commitment to provide for us and care for us. Jesus wanted to deal with the root cause because He must have seen that persistent worrying has the potential to cause a person great damage. A recent report from the Mental Health Foundation had this to say about the destructive effects of worrying:

Every system in your body is affected by worry. In addition to raising blood pressure and blood clotting, worrying can prompt your liver to produce more cholesterol – all of which can increase your risk of heart attack or stroke ... Muscle tension can give rise to headaches and back pain ... Worry can trigger an increase in stomach acid, and either slow or speed up muscle contraction in your intestines – which leads to stomach aches, constipation, diarrhoea, gas, or heartburn. Worry can affect your skin, causing rashes or itching. It can impact your respiratory system and can aggravate asthma, and growing evidence suggests that chronic worry can compromise your immune system making you more vulnerable to bacteria, viruses, and even cancer ...

142,000 people were admitted to hospital last year with deliberate self-harm. 19,000 of those were young people and it

is far more common for women to self-harm than men ... 75%
of all suicides are male ... 1 in every 4 people in our nation will
need some kind of mental, psychiatric or psychological help in
their life ... 1 in every 6 will have depression and it is most
common between the ages of 25 and 44. 1 in every 10 in
our population will suffer from disabling anxiety disorders ...
1 in every 100 will be schizophrenic or a manic depressive.

Even though women will have a higher ratio of mental illness
than men, men are three times more likely to have alcohol
dependency and twice as likely to be drug addicts.

Worry is one side effect of our fallen human nature. A
mind that is void of God's peace will not live in tranquillity,
but in apprehension of what lies around the next corner.
Arthur Somers Roche said that, "Worry is a thin stream of
fear trickling through the mind. If encouraged it cuts a
channel into which all other thoughts are drained." To give
in to worry is to take the line of least resistance. It is far
easier to let our emotions run wild than it is to have faith.
But if our minds are fixed on Christ then the power of
worry, anxiety and fear need not have dominion over us.
God's love releases the human mind to develop and grow in
the security of His presence. If Jesus told us to stop
worrying, then it must be within the grasp of human
thinking to change our thought patterns.

Even Elijah, that great man of faith and power, showed
signs of worry, anxiety and fear. Though he was often brave
and full of faith, he lived with a weakness. Though he would
readily stand in opposition against 400 men on another
occasion, he was afraid of a woman and fled for his life

(1 Kings 19). In verse 14 of this chapter we find Elijah alone and depressed: *"I alone am left; and they seek to take my life"* (NKJV). Yet he was not alone. There were still 7,000 people in Israel who had not bowed the knee to Baal! Fear and depression always distort the truth and make us believe that life's problems revolve around us. It was because of this incident that God called Elisha and trained him to be Elijah's replacement!

It is amazing to see the advice that the field of medicine goes on to give to those wishing to retain good mental health, and how closely that advice mirrors the wisdom of the Bible. Medical practitioners have identified three critical areas of development in a person's life that will contribute to a sound mind, and also three things that a person can initiate to prevent problems from occurring.

The most important thing we need to grasp as believers is that there are certain things that only we can do; they are not done for us, we must do them ourselves so that they form part of the spiritual disciplines of our walk with God. If you have appendicitis, then the doctor has to deal with it for you. If you have a heart attack, then somebody has to restore you. But with mental illness, there are certain things only you can do.

THREE AREAS OF DEVELOPMENT . . .

1. Develop emotionally

So often we create problems for ourselves because we allow our emotions to get out of control. If our emotions are allowed to run riot, they will constantly rise up and distort our normal thinking. So we need to develop our emotional life and learn to exert self-control when emotional highs and lows threaten to overwhelm us.

Once I was taking part in a wedding rehearsal where the bride-to-be was highly emotional. She came to me and said, "I don't know what to do. When I become emotionally charged about the wedding I either go into fits of hysterics or I weep uncontrollably." I said to her, "Don't worry, because on the day you won't do that." Surprised she asked, "Why?" I replied, "Because I'm in control of the wedding ceremony and I'm telling you sweetheart, you will not do that!" Guess what? On the big day, she didn't! Why? Essentially because I had given her permission to tell herself not to do that. I had shown her how to take authority over her emotions and she found she was quite capable of controlling them and not allowing them to get the better of her.

To develop emotionally means to develop creatively. Most people who become depressed and stay depressed sit down and do nothing. They allow their emotional life to shut down. If you are spiralling downward into depression, then begin to be creative! Start making something; start doing something that will shift the focus off you and your problems. We have had a number of people who were mentally ill come to our church looking for help. We usually say to them, come and do some voluntary work at the church, painting or something like that. Eventually, many of these people have been able to move forward and get themselves jobs. We were made to be like God, and God is a creative God. So start creating, start painting, whatever!

2. Develop intellectually

As well as developing emotionally, we need to develop intellectually. Stimulate your mind by studying and learning new things. The Bible says,

> *"Study and be eager and do your utmost to present yourself to God approved (tested by trial), a workman who has no cause to be ashamed, correctly analyzing and accurately dividing [rightly handling and skilfully teaching] the Word of Truth."*
>
> (2 TIMOTHY 2:15 AMP)

Get your mind active, begin to read, begin to write, go and study for further education, do something so that your mind is being exercised.

3. Develop spiritually

Bearing in mind that this advice originated from secular medicine, this is an incredible statement. Even our mental health institutions realise that you have a spirit – or at least acknowledge the existence of a spiritual dimension – and know that it must be nurtured. That's why it's important for you to be together with other Christians in church or in small groups – so that you are able to develop spiritually!

THREE THINGS TO INITIATE . . .

1. Face your problems

It's important for all of us to face our problems head on and not try to ignore them and hope they'll go away. You can't duck them or dodge them, and you can't blame anyone else. If you know you have a problem in a particular area, face up to it and say to yourself, "I'm not going to run away from this; I'm not going to put it down to the fact that I've always been like this; I'm not going to blame my family, my past, of anything else; I am going to face up to this and with God's help, overcome it."

It was the US president Harry S. Truman who invented the saying, "The buck stops here" and had it displayed on his desk for everyone to see. There has to be a time in your life when you don't "pass the parcel", but you actually "pass the test"!

2. Resolve your problems and learn from them

We are living in times when many people are mentally disturbed simply because they refuse to resolve their problems. People have a tendency not to put their problems to bed, learn from them and then move on. Some, for instance, will constantly fall in and out of relationships, either becoming abused by each successive partner, or alternatively being abusive to each new partner – all because they never seek to resolve or learn from their difficulties in relating to others and discussing their problems. Is this the same advice that God would give us? Yes! This is identical to the Bible.

3. Develop and sustain mutually satisfying personal relationships

Friendship does not come overnight. The Bible advises us that if we want to have friends then we are to go and be a friend to others. This is what God tells us to do and doctors are saying the same. You must take time to develop and build *mutually* – i.e. not just for your benefit – satisfying relationships. It's important that we don't spend all our time drawing resources out of other people. We have to be a giver as well as a receiver of friendship. There are too many people who just suck the life out of people until in the end their friends would rather pretend to be out than take their phone call.

Try to find friends who will gain something from having you in their presence. Do things that will cause them to say, "Man, you're such a good friend to me." If all you do is lean on people for help in a crisis, eventually you will kill their friendship and love towards you, simply because they can't cope any more. Be prepared to put in more than you will get out.

Learn New Habits

When it comes to worrying, statistics tell us that women are twice as likely as men to be affected by worry and related anxiety or panic disorders. Anxiety is cited as the number one problem amongst patients seeing a psychiatrist or psychologist. So what is the recommendation of our mental health institutions on how to deal with anxiety and worry? This is what the department of health says,

Worry is a habit. Learn new habits.

That is the full medical advice our government gives on protecting our mental health. It sounds very like the Bible to me:

"Be renewed in the spirit of your mind, and ... put on the new man which was created according to God, in true righteousness and holiness."

(EPHESIANS 4:23–24 NKJV)

"... flee these things and pursue righteousness, godliness, faith, love, patience, gentleness [develop godly habits and desires]*."*

(1 TIMOTHY 6:11 NKJV)

"... everyone who practices [makes a habit of] *righteousness is born of Him."*

(1 JOHN 2:29 NKJV)

✔ HEALTH CHECKLIST

Points covered in this chapter:

► God wants us to be whole people and a major key to our wholeness is peace of mind.

► Knowing this, Jesus gave this command to all believers of all times, "Do not worry." He went on to give specific examples of things we should not worry about, all of which are modern day preoccupations: our bodies, food, clothing.

► Worrying is just a symptom of something deeper. Fundamentally, it is a lack of confidence in God's ability to do what He has promised in caring and providing for us.

► There are three areas of development which can help us to become free from and avoid fear and anxiety: emotional, intellectual and spiritual.

► There are three things we can initiate in order to counteract anxiety before it grips us: face your problems; resolve your problems and learn from them; develop and sustain mutually satisfying personal relationships.

► Worrying is a habit. Learn new habits!

CHAPTER 5

TAKING YOUR THOUGHTS CAPTIVE

CATCH YOUR THOUGHTS EARLY

A key doctor in a recent medical report gave this advice on how to stop unhelpful thoughts getting out of control: "Catch your worrying early."

Let's see what the Bible says about this. In 2 Corinthians 10:5 we read,

"... casting down arguments and every high thing that exalts itself against the knowledge of God, bringing every thought into captivity to the obedience of Christ."

(NKJV)

So, our doctors are saying, "Catch your worrying thoughts early", but the apostle Paul is saying, "Catch every one!" Later he explains that the natural thoughts of a man "wage war" against God. In other words, any thought that doesn't originate from God (that is, a thought that would bring blessing to God and edification to us) is carnal and fleshly, and the flesh is always resistant to the purposes of God.

So what is a carnal thought? Let me give some examples of what it is *not*: it is not carnal to decide what colour to paint your front door – that's government. It is not carnal to decide whether to go on holiday to Los Angeles or Bognor Regis – that's common sense! (I won't tell you which one!) It is not carnal to decide whether to buy a 4-wheel drive car or a 2-wheel drive car – that's preference. Rather, any thought that plays to our base nature is carnal, and unless we take such thoughts captive, they will begin to destroy us – mentally, emotionally, spiritually and physically.

When you fall out with another person and don't deal with it, it destroys your relationship, destroys you as a person, and you lose trust and faith, so persistent carnal thoughts will gradually destroy you and erode your faith. Carnal thoughts have to be taken captive.

My wife and I have been married for thirty-four years. To say that during that time I have not noticed or seen some beautiful looking women wouldn't be true. If a man says that he has never been attracted by another woman, then his get up and go has got up and gone, or he never had it in the first place! No, it's what you do with those thoughts that counts. The doctors tells us to catch potentially damaging thoughts early and bring them under control, but Paul goes a step further than that, as we will see. It is no good simply catching your thoughts and taking them into captivity. If all you do is capture your thoughts, imprison them, and do nothing with them, then what you will end up with is a prison inside your mind. You may have taken those damaging thoughts captive, but they are still in your mind, lying dormant, waiting for an opportunity to resurface.

As long as you are harbouring carnal thoughts in your mind, even if they are not on the surface at present, there is always the danger of a breakout; and when those thoughts do manage to break out they will violate you. You may say, "Well, praise God I have never committed adultery. Those thoughts have come to me, but I've captured them", or "I've never fiddled the accounts yet, although I've had thoughts about it", but if you have only imprisoned those thoughts then they are still lurking in the background, ready to undermine you. You are kidding yourself that you are not wrestling with those thoughts every day. That's dangerous. All it takes is for something to trigger those thoughts and they will attack you again.

DON'T IMPRISON YOUR THOUGHTS, SENTENCE THEM TO DEATH

So what is Paul's solution to this problem? Our thoughts are not to be held in captivity for nothing. When you are arrested and charged there must be a court appearance, so our thoughts must be brought to trial. Policing your thoughts carefully is advantageous, but Paul says that every thought must be brought into captivity *to obedience in Christ.* In other words, we capture every thought and bring it in obedience to Christ to be judged. God then passes judgement on our thoughts for us and sentences to death every thought that didn't originate from Him.

I want the reader to understand, I am in no way glorifying war, but the SAS have a policy in war that is similar to what Paul is advocating for our thought life. Unless something goes wrong with an operation they are undertaking, the SAS never take any prisoners. They work on the assumption that, if you take prisoners, someone somewhere will eventually take reprisals and there will be a concerted effort to get the prisoners back.

I once interviewed a man who was one of the SAS personnel involved in the Iranian Embassy siege in London in 1980. He had become a vicar and later he tragically took his own life because he could not live with the things he had done whilst in active service. He told me that before the siege they had built an exact replica of the rooms in the embassy in a warehouse and had memorised every detail of the building, its furniture and its layout. They went into the real embassy with a single mandate – to take out every single terrorist and to take no prisoners.

In the event, there were two terrorists left alive after control of the embassy was regained and the hostages threatened to tell the press if the SAS killed them. So it was that they had to arrest the men, and months later other terrorists attempted to get them released by trying to hijack a plane. As I said, I have no desire to glorify war, but you can see the principle at work.

On one occasion, King Saul was commanded by the Lord to kill every man in an enemy army. He disobeyed, sparing the life of their king, and it caused Saul to fall into mental illness and eventually death. It is so important that we deal with our carnal thoughts according to the Bible-prescribed pattern. Thoughts that are "dead", can't come back to trouble you.

Paul says in 1 Corinthians 15:31, *"I die daily"* (NKJV). Paul was prepared to put his life on the line every day for the sake of the gospel, but he also recognised the value of dying to self so that God could have His way. Paul knew that if he didn't deal with his thoughts on a daily basis, then his thoughts would deal with him. He had conditioned his mind to continually bring his thoughts into obedience to Christ, so that anything not of God could be put to death.

RIGHT CHOICES AND WRONG CHOICES

The fact is, many Christians simply do not practise the biblical pattern of bringing their thoughts into obedience to Christ, and as a result their unchecked thought-life leads them into destructive behaviour. It happens gradually, subtly and eventually leads to disaster.

Why is it that so many men and women of God are committing adultery in these days? It is the result of a thought-life that has been allowed to breed one carnal thought after another without restraint. Numbers of great men of God have fallen from grace after committing adultery with women that they were meant to be counselling. The process happens something like this:

- *Day 1:*
  You come away from the counselling session thinking to yourself, "Do you know, I never realised that they were so stimulating to talk to. What a lovely personality they've got." The thought goes unchecked.

- *Day 2:*
  "You know, when we talk we've got a lot in common and I never thought we did."

- *Day 3:*
  "In a funny way, I don't mean sexually of course, they are quite attractive." Again the thought goes unchallenged.

- *Day 4:*
  "If my wife was no longer alive, God forbid, I think I could marry someone like her ... "

- *Day 5:*
  "I wish my wife wasn't around any more ... "

- *Day 6:*
  "If my wife wasn't around any more and I was a free man, this is what I would like to be doing with her ... "

- *Day 7:*
  You *are* doing it with her.

That is the power of the mind. That is how adultery starts. That is what leads up to someone coming to me and saying,

"Pastor David, I don't know how it happened." This is why, like Paul, we need to learn the art of dying daily. Using Paul's method, the thought process stops at, "Aren't they stimulating to talk to?" and it never gets any further.

We must die to any carnal thoughts that will invade our spirit and rise up against God. What does an alcoholic say? He says, "I didn't drink *today*." He lives each day, one day at a time. Similarly, we have to take control of our thoughts each day. Some people you meet have had their lives ruined because they have lived with unforgiveness in their minds for years. They should have given those thoughts up on the day they had them!

I once met a woman whose husband, the deputy governor of the Maize prison at the time, had been murdered. Four hooded men came to visit her husband while she was standing by holding their baby in her arms. He was leaving to go to work that morning and she told me that his kiss goodbye was still wet on her lips as he walked to his car. Seconds later four bullets hit him in the head and he was dead before he hit the floor. "I hid behind a car as they fired at me and the baby," she said. "When I went back into the house, I didn't even look back at my husband because I knew he had been transported to heaven." In that moment, she knew she had a decision to make. Was she going to forgive the men who had robbed her of her husband, and her baby of a father? "I made a conscious decision," she said, "that my mind would not be polluted by hatred and I forgave them then." Somehow she knew that if she didn't, she would live forever with bitterness and hate, even as a Christian. She made a conscious decision to die to those destructive thoughts.

So many people are mentally troubled and suffer depression because they continue to harbour destructive thoughts, instead of bringing them into obedience to Christ. Obedience means "compliant submission"; it means to agree to the command of God. If we keep our negative thoughts chained up, then we are not free. Bringing our thoughts into obedience to Christ destroys our wayward thoughts and the legal authority that Christ holds banishes confused minds. Instead, He leaves His peace with us and He is able to keep us in perfect peace if our minds are stayed (planted deeply, fixed) on Him.

Casting Down Thoughts Contrary to God

In life we are constantly faced with obstacles or thoughts that can rob us of the peace of God if we don't deal with them correctly. Whilst we must bring all our thoughts into obedience to Christ so that He can judge and sentence them accordingly, there are obstacles to right-thinking that we have to tear down ourselves. Paul says that we must "cast down" anything that is trying to captivate our thinking and is contrary to the knowledge of God (2 Corinthians 10:5).

What kind of things try to stifle the truth of God in our lives? You may say "I have a problem that goes back generations in my family. It might be a curse." It doesn't matter whether it's a curse, a generational trait, or just a bad attitude, you can cast it down. You must cast down all those images, false gods and strongholds which set themselves up in opposition to God.

Joshua issued this challenge to the people of Israel:

"Now therefore, fear the LORD, serve Him in sincerity and in truth, and put away the gods which your fathers served on the other side of the River and in Egypt. Serve the LORD! And if it seems evil to you to serve the LORD, choose for yourselves this day whom you will serve, whether the gods which your fathers served that were on the other side of the River, or the gods of the Amorites, in whose land you dwell. But as for me and my house, we will serve the LORD."

(JOSHUA 24:14–15)

You don't have to allow yourself to be dominated by the "gods of your father". Maybe your father was an alcoholic? Maybe you come from a long line of alcoholics? You have a choice: you can either live under that, or you can cast it down. Confront that thing and declare, "By the power of Christ, this is the last of the line of alcoholics in this family."

Too many people look for the easy way out. They want someone to come and pray for them that they will be delivered. No, says Paul, *you cast it down*. You! Don't take that stinking thing. King David went around the land casting down idols and you must do the same. It's you who has got to turn the TV off, burn all those books you shouldn't have, and throw those videos on the bonfire. It's you who have go to throw the bottles of booze out of your house. *You* have got to do that!

There are no easy answers when it comes to removing hindrances to your spiritual life. You will need to go around your house and take an inventory of what's there. Is there anything that is offensive to God; that is a hindrance to the knowledge of Him in your life? You will also need to take an inventory of your thought-life, your relationships, and maybe a few things will have to be thrown on the bonfire. You are going to have to arrest any unhelpful thought patterns, call the police of the Holy Ghost, and turn yourself in. Say to those negative, horrible thoughts: I'm turning you in.

THINGS YOU CAN DO TO AVOID WORRYING

Perhaps you are the kind of person who thinks, "This is all very well, but I just can't help worrying"? Well, you can. If secular medicine can say, "Catch your worrying early", and the apostle Paul can say, "Take your thoughts captive", and Jesus says, "Do not worry" – then be assured, you can stop worrying!

Jesus knows that you can stop worrying. If He knew that you had no ability to take control, then He would not command you to do it. Worry, like love, is based in the will – the thinking process of man. When Jesus commanded mankind, "You shall love the Lord your God with all your mind, spirit, emotions, and physical strength" He was asking us to make a conscious decision because love is an act of the will.

Some time ago, my wife and I exchanged cards. In hers, Molly had written, "We've had one of the worst years of our lives – I love you." It was true, all kinds of things had happened to us to attack us and wear us down. Sometimes life is tough and things are hard. When bad things happen, we don't try to put on a show – what you see is what you get

– but we refuse to allow those things to infiltrate who we are and distort our thinking and our relationship with God. No pastor is above the hardships of life and if they give you that impression then they are deceiving you! Ministers suffer the trials of life just like anyone else, but we go through them in order to show others that there is a way out if we change the way we think. Over the years, God has taught me to think in ways that I didn't even know I was capable of doing.

Jesus commanded us not to worry, but what was the context of that statement? If you examine the whole of Matthew chapter 6, it is interesting to note all the things that Jesus spoke about before coming to the conclusion, "Therefore I say to you, do not worry ... " The things that Jesus highlights beforehand are keys that will help us to take the focus off ourselves and will prevent us from becoming immersed in our own troubles.

1. Doing charitable deeds for people

Why would He say that? Because if you are being kind and loving to other people you are taking your mind off your own problems. That's why we (the church) go around ministering to the poor through "Helping Hands". You see some people who are in a terrible mess, with heavy duty problems. When you see how terrible it is for some people, you are really thankful that God has saved you and for what He's done in your life. When you start doing good to other people, you realise how much God has blessed you.

Jesus says, "Do good to others." Not to gain more brownie points, not to gain favour with God, but to stop focusing on yourself and to look outwards and not inwards. In addition to helping others, Jesus also stresses the importance of,

2. Praying
James 5:16 says,

> *"Confess your trespasses to one another, pray for one another, that you may be healed. The effective, fervent prayer of a righteous man avails much."*
>
> (NKJV)

Praying openly with others creates a unity and power that releases healing as we practise accountability in our relationships. In "confessing trespasses" we are not substituting others for the Lord. This is not referring to sin which should be confessed to God, but the wrong attitudes and wrong deeds we often commit against each other that, if not dealt with, cause disharmony and broken relationships.

3. Exercising forgiveness
In Matthew 6:9–13 we read about the model for prayer that Jesus established for His disciples: Jesus said, "Pray in this manner ..."

> *"Our Father in heaven,*
> *Hallowed be Your name.*
> *Your kingdom come.*
> *Your will be done*
> *On earth as it is in heaven.*
> *Give us this day our daily bread.*
> *And forgive us our debts,*

As we forgive our debtors.
And do not lead us into temptation,
But deliver us from the evil one.
For Yours is the kingdom and the power
      and the glory forever. Amen.

In this model prayer we see that only forgiveness is conditional. Unforgiveness disturbs the mind, brings death to the spirit and leaves the emotions embittered. When we forgive we do not justify the perpetrator or the act of offence, but we stand away from the seat of judgment, so releasing that person to the mercy and judgment of God and releasing ourselves from receiving their judgment. This is a vital key to mental wellbeing and the avoidance of worry. Matthew 7:1–2 confirms it:

"Judge not, that you be not judged. For with what judgment you judge, you will be judged; and with the measure you use, it will be measured back to you."

                                                  (NKJV)

4. Fasting

Fasting should never be legalistic, but is a time where we can replace food with the opportunity to seek the Lord for a breakthrough, just as Jesus did in the wilderness in Matthew chapter 4. Fasting should be carried out during a designated time set apart for one-to-one fellowship with God. It is good therapy to have regular set periods of time where we can be completely alone with God. Fasting should never been taken to extremes and if you are taking any kind of medication, clear it with your doctor before fasting.

5. Focusing on eternal rather than temporal values

"But seek first the kingdom of God and His righteousness, and all these things shall be added to you."

(MATTHEW 6:33 NKJV)

Jesus tells us to seek first the kingdom of God. In pursuing God's priorities above our own, we find that we gain assurance and confidence about our eternal future; we discover that we can entrust our daily worries and trials to the safe keeping of Jesus.

6. Guarding the eye gate

The Bible has much to say about "the eyes" both literally and metaphorically. In Luke 6:42 Jesus advises that we should deal with our own problems before we go criticising others for theirs:

"How can you say to your brother, 'Brother, let me remove the speck that is in your eye,' when you yourself do not see the plank that is in your own eye? Hypocrite! First remove the plank from your own eye, and then you will see clearly to remove the speck that is in your brother's eye."

(NKJV)

Jesus taught that what we allow in through our eyes is very important. If we are careful to monitor the things we choose to focus on, then it will help us to maintain our purity:

"The lamp of the body is the eye. If therefore your eye is good, your whole body will be full of light."

(MATTHEW 6:22 NKJV)

Revelation 3:18 speaks of anointing your eyes with salve. It is metaphorical language that means we need to let the Holy Spirit touch the eyes of our understanding, enabling us to have a vision for our life that is in line with what God sees. It allows us to see God's perspective. Such a perspective will set us free from the bondage of worry, anxiety and fear.

✔ HEALTH CHECKLIST

Points covered in this chapter:

▶ Medical experts advise people to "catch their worrying early" mirroring the biblical wisdom of "taking your thoughts captive".

▶ Ungodly thoughts must be captured early on and dealt with swiftly. Unchecked thoughts remain dormant in the mind and wait for an opportunity to resurface.

▶ Carnal thoughts are not to be merely imprisoned, but brought into obedience to Christ and put to death. Wrong choices are made when sinful thoughts are allowed to linger in the mind.

▶ In Matthew chapter 6 Jesus highlights six things you can do to stop worrying and focus your thoughts in the right direction: doing charitable deeds for others; praying; exercising forgiveness; fasting; focusing on eternal rather than temporal values; guarding the eye gate.

CHAPTER 6

THE BATTLE
FOR THE MIND

At times our minds can be so deceived that we can be the last person to really understand ourselves. We are our own best friend and worst enemy at the same time. One of the hardest things in the world for anyone to do, is to see themselves as they really are and as other people see them. The great Scottish poet Robert Burns once wrote, "O, wad some Power the giftie gie us, to see oursels as others see us!"[1] Actually, there is such a Power that can give us the gift to see ourselves as we really are – His name is the Holy Spirit.

Your mental view of yourself tends to be made up of three parts: there is the person that *you think you are*; the person you let *other people think you are*; and there's the person *that you really are.* This means that our self-view is often distorted and out of balance – we either think too highly of ourselves or too lowly of ourselves. The Holy Spirit however, can help us to face up to the truth about ourselves, both good and bad, and to get the balance right. Only the Spirit can reveal to us how God sees us and give us an understanding of how we are to see ourselves in the light of that. Although we are fallen, failing, weak human beings, God looks on us with the eyes of love. That's why He sent His Son to die for us.

DOUBLE-MINDEDNESS

I believe that a major reason for people having a flawed image of themselves is what the Bible calls double-mindedness. A psychologist might call this condition "schizophrenia" in its most extreme form, but before such mental health concepts were thought of, the apostle James (in the context of faith) warned us about, *"... a double-minded man, unstable in all his ways"* (James 1:8 NASB) and later commanded us, *"Purify your hearts, you double-minded"* (James 4:8 NKJV). The psalmist also wrote, *"I hate double-minded men"* (Psalm 119:113 NIV).

The Bible is very clear that confusion of the mind – double-mindedness – leads to only one thing: instability, and not just in some areas, but in *"... **all** his ways".* When a person is in a state of double-mindedness they cannot think single-mindedly about anything – God, their relationships, their work etc. If a person is "unstable" it doesn't neces-sarily means that they are collapsing now, but eventually something will happen to bring about the breakdown that has been waiting to happen. When you walk over a bridge that is unstable, for instance, it doesn't mean that it is broken – but it could break at any time, with disastrous consequences. Just because you are not having a breakdown in your life right now, does not mean you are not unstable. It just takes the right kind of crisis-trigger to send us over the edge.

The Mind Affects Your Whole Being

To have a sound mind is of critical importance, because the state of your mind will dictate your overall wellbeing. If your mind is contaminated, then your whole being is affected. Although we think of the mind as being a small part of us, it affects our whole person and everything we do. There is a true story of a plane that could have exploded killing hundreds of people and causing untold damage, if it wasn't for the vigilance of one person:

A number of planes were queued up ready for take off and the pilot of one of them noticed that, as the plane in front of him took off, it was leaking aviation fuel which was flowing out of the back of it. Quickly, he radioed the pilot and told him he was losing fuel and the airline declared an emergency. The plane was scheduled for the West Indies, so they flew over the North Sea and jettisoned two-thirds of their fuel, then returned to the airport and managed to make a safe landing. All this happened because a maintenance man left off a tiny plate a few inches across, putting the screws that should hold it in place nearby in a plastic bag. It took one small plate to make a whole passenger jet extremely unstable and dangerous. It's just the same with our minds.

THE X-FACTOR

Recently, I watched some of the series *The X-Factor* with my daughter. For anyone who didn't see it, it was the latest in a long line of reality TV shows, and the idea was to give people of all ages the opportunity to audition to become a "star" by singing in front of a panel of experts. I watched it because I thought to myself, "This could actually prove the point I am writing about."

The show is structured in such a way that it encourages you to fall about in hysterics over how bad the contestants are – how terribly they sing, or how badly they put themselves across. But the really tragic thing about it is, every one of the people who turned up to audition, sincerely believed that they could sing and "make it" as a top entertainer. They simply could not analyse what was coming out of their mouths in an objective way.

Basically these people were deceived in their minds. Everyone who listens to them knows that they are embarrassing themselves, but they don't seem to realise that or hear how bad they are. Many of us find their lack of realisation incredible, and yet, all of us without exception, suffer from that exact problem too – to one degree or another! We all live under that deception.

You hear people saying all the time, "Well, I'm not as bad as that person ..." Pardon? Do you not see what the rest of us see? Often in churches you will get the person who approaches you and says, "I should be in charge of the music group" when clearly they should not. Anyone who has stood next to them in a service knows that they are tone deaf! They are living under a deception. Maybe you've lived with the thought that you should have been a professional footballer if only you'd been given the right breaks? But the reality is, you weren't good enough. That's not negativism, it's reality, and you must face up to it and move on with your life.

The Deceitfulness of the Heart

So, why do we persist with such thoughts and continue to create a flawed image of ourselves? The prophet Jeremiah gives us a clear answer:

> *"The heart is deceitful above all things,*
> *And desperately wicked;*
> *Who can know it?"*
>
> (JEREMIAH 17:9 NKJV)

You don't need medical or psychiatric training, or a diploma in counselling to unlock the problem of double-mindedness. The Bible pinpoints the problem immediately – the human heart is naturally deceitful.

"Who can understand the human heart?" Jeremiah cries. Certainly not us, because we are the last ones to realise how deceived we are!

The next verse is even more troubling:

> *"I, the LORD search the heart,*
> *I test the mind,*

Even to give every man according to his ways,
According to the fruit of his doings."

(JEREMIAH 17:10 NKJV).

Here we see that God searches the spiritual content of our hearts and tests our minds. Jeremiah says that God will give us "the fruit" – that is, the results – of the way in which we think, according to what is in our heart. The apostle Paul reflects this truth later in Romans when he says of those whose hearts and minds are far away from God,

". . . as they did not like to retain God in their knowledge, God
gave them over to a debased mind, to do those things which are
not fitting."

(ROMANS 1:28 NKJV).

In other words, God says to us, "If you insist on following the path of a deceived mind, then I will give you over to that deception. Whatever way of thinking you want to have, I will release you into it!" That is a sobering, frightening thought and it shows us why having a sound mind, surrendered to God, is so important.

Doesn't it strike you as ironic that the expert panel on the *X-Factor* was getting paid to tell people the truth about themselves? If you did that in church, everybody would leave! The world is such an upside-down place! The world gets paid to tell people the truth while the church gets paid to lie! How many ministers spend all their time pandering to their congregation and telling them what they want to hear; what will make them feel good about themselves? The answer is, plenty – because if they told them the hard truth, half the congregation would be gone overnight. Yet, Jesus instructed us to tell the truth, but in love.

Once a group of five young men came up to me and said, "Pastor David, will you speak into our lives? Tell us the truth about ourselves because we want to change and be used by God." I said to them, "Do you really want to hear the truth about yourselves?" "Yes," they replied. So, I did: "This is what's wrong in your life ... this is where you need to change ..." Out of the five young guys stood before me, only two could tolerate hearing the truth about themselves and the others gradually left. Why? Because what they actually wanted was endorsement, not truth. They wanted me to confirm for them the things that they thought about themselves. I have many failings, but never ask me what I really think about you, because I will tell you!

THE PEACE OF GOD

Somebody has got to tell us the truth about ourselves, otherwise we will live our whole lives under an illusion. The Holy Spirit will help us here as long as we submit to His rule in our lives and allow Him to search our hearts. Once an issue is brought to the surface and we acknowledge our need for the Father to deal it, it can be dealt with successfully. We will however, continue to struggle with many issues whilst they remain buried inside of us.

Thankfully, God has made a wonderful provision for us which means we don't have to live with our minds in constant turmoil. Paul writes in Philippians,

"The peace of God, which surpasses all understanding, will guard your hearts and minds through Christ Jesus."

(PHILIPPIANS 4:7 NKJV)

God's peace, which surpasses all reasoning and understanding, can put a guard on your heart and mind if you belong to Jesus. When you have submitted your mind to the peace of God, He puts a sentry around your heart, just as He placed a sentry to guard the garden of Eden. And when God places a guard, woe betide anyone who tries to get past it! The peace of God brings balance to the mind. It stops you from having emotional hallucinations about yourself – either thinking you are a lot worse than you actually or, or thinking you are much better than you actually are.

Receiving the peace of God is a supernatural act, accomplished by the Holy Spirit living inside you as you surrender to God's will and purposes for transforming your character. There is no intellectual formula for it; you cannot attain the peace of God through biblical study or academic learning alone. It is an experience born out of a relationship with God that impregnates your being. Jesus said these comforting words,

"Peace I leave with you, My peace I give to you; not as the world gives do I give to you. Let not your heart be troubled, neither let it be afraid."

(JOHN 14:27 NKJV)

He promised peace of mind to all those who would abide in Him. It is this fact of being *at peace* with God that *becomes* the peace of God within us. It is the amazing and overwhelming peace of God that caused the hymn writer to write,

My sin, oh, the bliss of this glorious thought!
My sin, not in part but the whole,
Is nailed to the cross, and I bear it no more,
Praise the Lord, praise the Lord, O my soul!

It is well, with my soul,
It is well, with my soul,
It is well, it is well, with my soul.[2]

When a man is at peace with God he sings of the "bliss" of that "glorious thought"; when a man is at peace with God he is no longer in mental turmoil. Most of the times in life when we are down on ourselves or we fall out with other people, it because we are not happy people – we are not at peace with ourselves because we are not at peace with God. Even Christians fall out with one another and leave churches. Why? Because they are not at peace, not content with their lives. But God's peace can guard and protect your heart and mind.

When it comes to peace of mind, self-effort will do you no good. It's no good *trying* not to think a certain way – you must have the peace of God which comes supernaturally. In other words, you've got to have a spiritual transformation before you can have a mental transformation. We are born again of the Spirit, and then we have our minds renewed. It has to happen in that order, so that our renewal is God's responsibility to bring about; it is not something we can achieve through intellectual application.

No one ever became a Christian because they were clever. You become a Christian because you are repentant. When you are born again the Holy Spirit effectively speaks to your mind and says, "You better get renewed, I'm not having a dirty mind representing Me to the world." So your spirit tells your mind, "Get yourself sorted out!"

If a person is bitter and twisted, living in deception, that tells you a lot about their spirit. If a person has a bitter spirit, it will affect the way they think and behave towards others. And having "acted out" or confessed that bitterness, that person will become ever more what they confess, becoming increasingly bitter in a downward spiral. But when you have a spirit that is yearning after God, it will nag your mind into submission. Your spirit within you cries out, "I'm not prepared to live in this depression and negativity any more! I'm not prepared to listen to gossip any more! I won't listen to you!"

Your spirit wars with your flesh to surrender to God and co-operate with His will. Many of the Greek words in the Bible for "flesh" also mean "mind". So when Paul talks of the battle between the spirit and the flesh he is not saying that it's your physical body that declares war on your spiritual life, it's your mind. The mind must be brought into submission and it is a war!

KEEPING THE PEACE OF GOD

The apostle Paul has some specific advice for us that will help us to keep the peace of God in our hearts and minds. It is a question of what we choose to focus on. Are we constantly dwelling on things that will destroy the peace of

God in our life, or are we dwelling on things that will keep the peace of God and even multiply it?

Having told us that the peace of God is capable of guarding our hearts and minds, he tells us,

> *"Finally, brethren, whatever things are true, whatever things are noble, whatever things are just, whatever things are pure, whatever things are lovely, whatever things are of good report, if there is any virtue and if there is anything praiseworthy – meditate on these things. The things which you learned and received and heard and saw in me, these do, and the God of peace will be with you."*
>
> (PHILIPPIANS 4:8–9 NKJV)

"Finally … whatever things are true …" Let's stop right there! "Finally," says Paul, "Let's sort out what is true." It's no good having a guard around your heart if you are going to follow lies. Ask the Holy Spirit to help you to begin to find out what is true about you, what's true about what God thinks about you, and what's true about the circumstances you find yourself in.

We can also focus on things that are noble, says Paul. Noble – what a lovely word – it means upright, dignified, of royal blood, something that is regal.

Nobility is a concept that the world today would do well to recapture. God wants to bestow nobility upon His children. Think about a single woman who really longs to be with someone. Maybe she has been used and abused and left hurting; told that she is a nobody. Now she's alone, so perhaps she thinks, "What's the point of dressing up when there's nobody here to see me?" In Christ that woman can brush her hair, put her makeup on and think, "I'm noble this morning."

I used to be a salesman and worked from home most of the time. Most people who have worked from home for any length of time will tell you that a good way to approach your working day is to get up, have a shower, put your business suit and tie on, and go to your desk as if you were going to your office. What a load of piffle you might think! But when I was in sales, I tried conducting my business unshaven, wearing a pair of jeans and I could never get an appointment to see a potential customer! Then I tried getting up in the morning and taking the time to put my suit on and groom myself ready for the day's business. The client still couldn't see me, but I could see me! I felt noble and it worked!

At first my wife would say to me,

"Where are you going?"

"Nowhere," I would reply.

"Well, why are you getting dressed up then?"

"I've got to make some phone calls."

Is that stupid? No it's not. It's simple psychology. If you dress like a bum, then you think like a bum. Rather, focus on that which is noble.

Paul goes on to make a number of further recommendations: "whatever things are *just*, whatever things are *pure*, whatever things are *lovely*, whatever things are of *good report*" – not negative, not gossip, but of good report. Listen to good news not bad news. "If there is any virtue in anything, if there is anything praiseworthy, meditate on it" – chew it like a cow chews the cud; keep turning those things over in your mind and you won't finish up depressed.

This scripture has a direct link with Galatians 5:22–23 which says,

"The fruit of the Spirit is love, joy, peace, longsuffering, kindness, goodness, faithfulness, gentleness, self-control. Against such there is no law."

(NKJV)

I preach all over the country. If you can't get anybody saved when you preach, what you can do to get an altar call is say, "Is there anybody here who feels rejected, lonely, stabbed in the back? Has anyone been spoken about badly, misunderstood?" By golly, it's a good job you are on the platform when you give such an appeal, otherwise you would suffocate!

I have suffered with all those things myself in my time, but do you know what? I don't go out for ministry to have them dealt with. Not because I'm proud, but because I dealt with them at the time when they happened. I've been a pastor for thirty-three years. During that time I've been spat on, weed on from a great height, sometimes by my own friends and family. But guess what? I'm still free from self-pity, rejection and loneliness.

THE PROTECTION OF THE ARMOUR OF GOD

So far Paul has given us two essential tools that we can use to protect and preserve our mental wellbeing – supernaturally receiving the peace of God, and focusing on positive, healthy things that will keep us in that place of peace. Then in Ephesians, Paul encourages us to put in place one further piece of protection to ensure that our minds are safe and secure.

In Ephesians chapter 6 we read some familiar verses about putting on what Paul describes as "the armour of God". He uses the analogy of the armour of a Roman soldier to highlight the importance of abiding in Christ and so having the spiritual protection we need, especially for those areas which are easily attacked, and not least our minds.

The covering provision of the armour of God is mainly for three areas vulnerability in man:

1. *Our minds*. The helmet of salvation is for the protection of the mind – our thinking capacity.

2. *Our hearts*. The breastplate of righteousness is for the protection of the heart – our emotional capacity.

3. *Our sexuality*. The "skirt" or belt of truth is for the protection of our sexuality.

These are three areas in which all of us are notoriously weak. It is easy for anyone to be tripped up and fall in one of these areas, and as one area is breached, so the next is liable to attack. People who commit adultery for instance, begin by allowing their thoughts about another person go unchecked. One that has happened the next step is for the heart to become involved, and once the heart has been persuaded that a certain course of action is right, then our sexuality is allowed to take over and we fall.

Man's sexuality needs the cover of God's truth; the heart needs to maintain righteousness, and the mind needs to be protected. If you can keep yourself sexually pure, with a heart that is righteous, and a mind that is whole, then you can do anything and accomplish great things for God.

Paul speaks about protecting our head – our mind – with salvation. In the Greek, salvation and wholeness are the same word, and both essentially mean "healing". Our minds need a twofold application:

1. *We need to have our minds "redeemed" from their previous fallen state*. Salvation moves us from our previous fallen state and brings us into a present state of stability. Another meaning of the word salvation is "to pluck out of". Being saved is literally like being plucked out of a burning building – one moment your life was in peril and now you are safe.

2. *Our minds need healing*. The covering of salvation for our minds means the restoration of a broken or destroyed mindset. When God saves you and you puts the helmet of salvation on, He takes you from danger and puts you into safety; He takes you from failure and puts you into security and then healing comes and He deals with the damage in your thinking and emotions that you have suffered because of sin.

Remember the story of the demoniac legion whom Jesus healed? He was a man so demonised that it affected him physically – he had to be chained up for his own safety and the safety of others; morally – he was naked; and mentally – his condition had driven him out of his mind.

Legion was mentally deranged, spiritually possessed, and morally destitute – until Jesus spoke to him. When Jesus got out of the boat and approached the man, the demons instantly knew who He was, and that they were in trouble! The demons cried out, "Have you come to persecute us?" And Jesus said, "Shut up!" Don't you just love Jesus when He's rude?! Have you come to persecute us? Yes! Next question! There were a lot of demons to come out, but Jesus didn't cast them out over a dozen sessions of counselling and sixteen boxes of Kleenex! He just said, "Come out!" and they went.

The demons went and the man was found *sitting* at the feet of Jesus – that's a metaphor for a spiritual experience. The renewal of the mind must start in your spirit. There must be a heart that is hungering for God before the mind can be straightened out. The man previously known as "legion" was now "clothed and in his right mind". How did he get those clothes? They didn't just appear, so the disciples must have given him them to him. The helped to restore his morality. The flesh had been dealt with and now he was in his right mind.

That is how we are meant to be – in possession of a sound mind. We must remember, greater is He that is in us than he that is in the world. We have got to declare war on the demonic and war on mental illness. Put on the whole armour of God so that you will be able to stand and do battle against the evil one. Let's be a people who think straight. Learning how to be truthful with God, yourself, and other people by submitting to the Holy Spirit is a good place to start.

✔ HEALTH CHECKLIST

Points covered in this chapter:

▶ One of the hardest things for anyone to do is to see themselves as they really are. The reason for our flawed self-image is double-mindedness, but the Holy Spirit can reveal the truth of how God sees us.

▶ The state of our mind will affect our whole being. If the mind is contaminated, then the whole person is affected.

▶ We struggle to understand ourselves because the human heart is naturally deceitful. Often we do not truly know what is in our own heart. The Holy Spirit can help us break out of this and receive the truth of God's Word if we submit our minds to His rule.

▶ The Bible teaches that the peace of God which surpasses all understanding can put a guard around your heart and mind like a sentry guarding a doorway.

▶ Receiving the peace of God is a supernatural act accomplished by surrendering to the Holy Spirit. It cannot be attained by mental assent, but is born out of a relationship with God that impregnates your being.

▶ You can learn to "keep" the peace of God by focusing on that which is true, noble, just, lovely, of good report, virtuous and praiseworthy (Philippians 4:8–9).

▶ The covering of the armour of God in Ephesians 6 is designed to protect our minds, our hearts, and our sexuality.

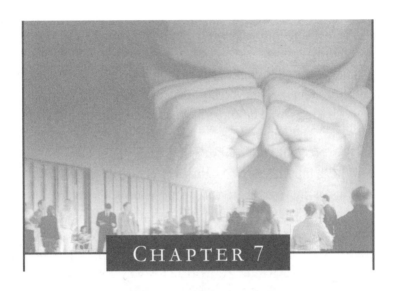

CHAPTER 7

AS A MAN THINKS IN HIS HEART ...

THOUGHTS BECOME BELIEFS AND BELIEFS TURN INTO ACTIONS

From the heart of every person outside of Christ come questions about the meaning of life. From deep within, the soul of man cries out for answers: "Why am I here? Am I going to die? What happens after death?" The mind of man can only answer those questions by turning to human philosophy or sociology, trying, like a computer, to process all the available information it can to find an answer to the problem.

The Bible however, tells us that man's intellectual capacity alone will never be able to uncover the answers he is looking for. The most revealing scripture is found in Proverbs 23:7 which says, *"As he thinks in his heart, so is he"* (NKJV). Note that it doesn't say, "As he thinks in his *mind* ... ", but "his heart" – the very centre of his being.

What is in your heart will shape you as a person. The content of your heart governs what you believe, and whatever you truly believe, you will act upon. What comes out of your heart is a breathtakingly potent force that shapes your behaviour. Heart-belief is why a man who has earned himself a PhD can still think of himself as a failure – because that's what he believes about himself inside.

What makes a football team play badly for one manager and then suddenly win six matches in a row for another manager? It's nothing to do with ability; it's nothing to do with a change of personnel; it's to do with a change in their thinking and a new self-belief in their hearts. A new manager can release in his team the possibility of being winners instead of losers. The players are no better than they were before, but suddenly they are motivated to perform to a new level, because now they believe in their hearts that they can do it!

The fact is, all our successes and failures in life start with a thought. An idea enters our mind and it conceives the possibility of a reality. Once a thought becomes embedded in our heart it will eventually lead to action, because we act based on our beliefs. It is what we *do* with our thoughts in life that really counts – especially those thoughts that are sinful and not of God. Some time ago, one of my best friends in the ministry for over twenty years, committed adultery. How did that process start? In started in his head. He had a decision to make: whether to put to death distracting, lustful thoughts, or whether to dwell on them and allow them to penetrate his heart. Once he had allowed himself to meditate on those thoughts, sin was conceived in his heart, and after that had happened, it wasn't long until his actions turned it into a reality.

It is very rare that a man or woman will immediately fall in love with someone at first sight. The world would like us to believe it's possible, but that's rubbish! What is possible is "lust at first sight". The first time you see or meet a person, you don't know what love is – it's all about physical attraction. That's the lust of the flesh: a man wanting a woman or a woman wanting a man. Love is far deeper than that. It has to be conceived and have a period of gestation before it grows into anything.

Therefore, if a married person brings their thoughts under control at the point where they find another man or woman (apart from their spouse) physically attractive, then it will prevent adultery from taking place. You decide with your mind what you allow into your heart; and what you allow into your heart is actually what takes you over.

THE POWER OF CONFESSION

You don't have to look too hard in life to see just how true the Bible is when it says, *"As a man thinks in his heart, so is he."* I often say that I love people to lose their tempers! Actually, it shouldn't be called "losing your temper" it should be called "telling the truth"! Because when people get angry and emotional they will often reveal the true feelings of their heart. When people have arguments they will make up by saying, "I'm sorry, I shouldn't have said that", but really, they should have said it – because that's what they really believe!

We are such complex and devious beings that often we will seek to suppress the true feelings in our heart. Our minds will keep a lid on our heart, saying, "You can't tell them what you really feel – it'll get you into trouble" or "you mustn't say that – it will hurt their feelings." Eventually however, usually in a time of vulnerability, the true feelings of our heart will spill out. Our heart says to our mind, "Move over, it's my turn now" and out comes all the garbage! It is usually when we realise what damage that can do that we backtrack by saying, "I'm sorry, I didn't mean it . . . " But the fact is, you did mean it because it was in your heart.

I used to work as an interrogator. Some people say I still do! I was involved in questioning people who had stolen money by committing fraud. My partner and I used to do a hard man/soft man routine just like the FBI! My job sometimes was to push people to breaking point so that they suddenly lost their temper and told me the truth. I would keep on goading them for a long period of time and then the soft man would come in and be sympathetic with them. Sometimes I would play the soft man for a while myself, and then revert to being the hard man again. After sustained pressure, someone would say something and "boom" out it would all come. Eventually what is hidden in the heart will come out.

There is incredible power in confession. The Bible speaks about it all the time. Eventually you are bound to confess whatever is in your heart. The mind is the servant of the heart. What we say with our mouths is often either a binding or a releasing factor. As thoughts become embedded in your heart, and you begin to speak out and confess what you believe, the creative power of your words reinforces the beliefs that are in your heart. The heart believes, but it is the mouth that creates the cradle which rocks the baby! Our words only help to reinforce our positive or negative attitudes.

When you hear people saying things like, "I'm no good ... I'm a failure", then they will be! How about this one: "All the men in our family have been alcoholics, so I daresay I will be too." Guess what? You probably will be if that is your confession, because your confession reveals your inner belief. The thought started in your mind, you allowed it to penetrate your heart, and now that you are confessing it you are solidifying it, feeding it. If you are going to consistently speak out negative things about yourself then you might as well give up now! Inevitably you will begin to identify with the words you are speaking about yourself and you will become what you speak.

Time and again people who have fallen into sin will say, "I couldn't help myself" or "I don't know what came over me." But they do know what came over them! They thought it, conceived it, confessed it and eventually did it. If you are thinking about sin, then it's only a matter of time. If you are thinking that one day you will probably become an alcoholic, it's a matter of time. As a man thinks in his heart, so is he.

When you allow wrong thoughts to consistently invade your mind it places a filter over the lens of your perception. Your view of situations is coloured. According to your particular filter then different aspects of the "picture" you see will be accentuated. In such a situation the panoramic teachings of Christ will become distorted by your emotional or mental state. Our thought processes must be constantly exposed to the regenerating power of the Holy Spirit.

A long time ago I stopped confessing that I was a failure. I've even stopped confessing that I don't know why God loves me – something that many Christians do all the time. I know why God loves me – because God loves everybody! Because it's nothing to do with me – it's all to do with Him. I've started confessing that it's God's love for me that has changed me, not my love for Him.

As a child I had great difficulty in retaining information. In the 1950s dyslexia was not commonly understood. Words like "thick" or "stupid" were the technical term given to people like me. Leaving school with no qualifica-tions, no self-confidence, self-esteem, and no reading or writing skills, I often cried myself to sleep at night or found myself in a state of extreme anger or fear.

It was only when I was born again and filled with the Holy Spirit that my ability to retain and use information changed. God supernaturally gave me the ability to learn rapidly and to retain and translate information into workable life skills. God had completely renewed my mind, and over time He taught me the importance of having a positive confession and of aligning myself with the truth of His Word.

Peter, who was a temperamental fisherman with little or no education, sat for three years under the teaching of Jesus, listening but often not fully understanding. His personality was a bit strange. I describe him as temperamental – full of temper and a little bit mental! Yet, after being filled with the Holy Spirit he delivered one of the most theologically sound sermons ever preached! The Holy Spirit renews the mind and changes our ability to reason and comprehend. Perfect peace of mind is guaranteed if we keep our minds fixed on Jesus.

Job was a man chosen by God to be tested by Satan. All hell broke loose on Job's life as he lost his financial security, his children and finally his health. In Job 2:10 we read that, *"In all this Job did not sin with his lips"* (NKJV). It looks at first as though Job will have a great mental attitude towards his situation, despite being surrounded by the negativity of his friends. But only a few verses later we read, *"After this Job opened his mouth and cursed the day of his birth."* For the next twenty-four verses he sinks into despair and fear:

> *"The thing I greatly feared has come upon me,*
> *And what I dreaded has happened to me.*
> *I am not at ease, nor am I quiet;*
> *I have no rest, for trouble comes."*
>
> (JOB 3:25–26 NKJV).

Job's confession has compounded his state of mind. Here is a man who is now fully depressed, restless, in dread of what could happen next and utterly robbed of peace. We have to understand that our mouths can talk us in or out of victory! Paul said,

> *"I can do all things through Christ who strengthens me."*
> (PHILIPPIANS 4:13 NKJV)

In Christ we live in a "can do" culture! I can become an overcomer; I can run and not grow weary; I can rise up on wings like an eagle; I can and I will! Confession is important, so make sure that yours is positive, bringing blessing to your life and not bondage.

THE POWER
OF CIRCUMSTANCES

Have you noticed that when things go wrong in our lives, we always blame circumstances? Much like the person who says, "I don't know what came over me" you can often sit down and listen to someone give you numerous reasons why a particular situation has arisen in their life. "Let me tell you *why* this happened," they say, and you listen to their story waiting for the punch line, which never comes: "Well Pastor David, I started drinking because ... first of all I lost my job ... then the car had to go back ... then my wife left me ... etc." Although these are heart-breaking circumstances, they are not the reason this person started drinking. The cause of that lies somewhere much deeper.

Any lawyer will tell you that you cannot convict someone based on circumstantial evidence. Circumstantial evidence may be complicit in a crime, but it can't convict you. You can only be convicted on the basis of facts and evidence; circumstantial evidence cannot be proven.

Circumstances are just part of the build up to a problem. A driver who is caught speeding can say, "A guy pulled out of a side road dangerously and I had to speed up to avoid being hit by him", or perhaps, "I was distracted by a low-flying plane", but all the police will be interested in is the fact that you were doing 60 in a 30 zone when they pulled you over! Forget the rest – you broke the law! People use circumstantial evidence as an attempt to get off with a lighter penalty, but the fact is – you were driving too fast!

If you think about it, people blame their circumstances all the time. They will say that their childhood experiences made them the way they are – that the way they were brought up ruined any chance of them living a successful life. One meaning of the word "circumstance" is "the logical surrounding of an action". We take that to heart when we say, "Here's what I did, and here are the reasons why it is logical that I did it!" But wait! What is logical to you is not necessarily logical to me. Listen to the discussions any group of fans will have after a football match: one will say, "They shouldn't have taken him off" and another will say, "They should never have brought him on!" A dozen different fans will all contradict one another. So what is logic? Logic is a human understanding of man's frailty. There is no such thing as logic! I think it's entirely logical that people should believe in God, but other people don't. You can't depend on logic, because logic changes with new evidence.

A "circumstance" is also defined as "an attendant fact". When you go to a wedding there may be any number of beautiful bridesmaids there who are looking really lovely, but guess what? Nobody comes to a wedding to see the bridesmaids. They are attendant to the fact of the wedding, but without the bride there will be no wedding.

So it may be true that you had problems in your

upbringing; that you didn't have good schooling; that you had no money; that you had a bad start in life. But all these things are like the bridesmaids at a wedding. They are not the main event. What you are and the way you behave is governed by what you have allowed to take root in your heart. Those things will dictate your behaviour and shape your life.

Circumstantial evidence is only the frame – it's not the picture. What is the picture of your life? Forget about the frame, because you can alter that; what is the main picture? With God's power we can rise above the circumstances of life and still radiate His light and love to others. The circumstances we are in are just attendant facts – they are not the main event.

People often talk about "circumstances" in negative terms: "I'm OK – under the circumstances" etc. But if you are a believer and your life is in God's hands, then you have to believe that He has your best interests at heart and that the circumstances of your life are allowed by Him, so that He can reveal more of Himself to you. What may seem to be "coincidences" to some people are actually "God-incidents" that He will use to accomplish something for us, or for someone else through us.

I once was asked to speak at a crusade in Ireland and while I was there was invited to pray for a number of sick people. Someone approached me and asked if I would visit their neighbour in hospital who was dying. He had cancer in both lungs, his kidneys and liver were infected, and he was in great pain.

I agreed to go and see the man and when I arrived at the hospital, they brought us together in a private family room.

I went in to the room and for some reason I left the door slightly ajar. I put my hand on this man and I prayed for him that God would heal him. The very next day his wife arrived at the evening meeting where I was speaking and came to talk to me. She said, "Pastor David, I was due to bring my husband home next week so that he could die in his own home. He phoned me half an hour after you had gone and said that after you put your hand on his back and prayed in the name of Jesus, a warmth went right through his body and all the pain went." I had prayed for him on a Thursday. By Friday morning his kidneys had begun working again under their own action, and shortly after that his liver was free from any infection. The doctors were so puzzled that they did a scan on him and found that the tumours on his lungs had shrunk dramatically.

As I was praying in that small room, a lady had walked in seeing that the door was slightly open. She was very apologetic for disturbing us, but I reassured her that it was no problem. But then she recognised me – she had seen my picture on a poster advertising the crusade. The result was that I ended up praying for her husband who was dying. Her husband was in a bed just around the corner from where we were. He too would have been sent home to die already, had it not been for the fact that there was a delay in preparing his medication to send home with him. These were just the circumstances as far as I was concerned, but the fact was God wanted to touch that woman and her husband and He engineered the circumstances to fulfil His purpose. That's why we should never despise our circumstances, but rather allow God to work out His will and purpose through them.

WHERE IS YOUR MIND FIXED?

In Romans 8:4–5 Paul gives us this advice,

> *"... do not walk according to the flesh but according to the Spirit. For those who live according to the flesh set their minds of the things of the flesh, but those who live according to the Spirit, the things of the Spirit."*

(NKJV)

That word "fix" means to stabilise, to solidify. There are two camps of people – those whose mind is fixed on this world and those whose mind is fixed on God. Those whose minds are set on the things of this world are being tormented continually by them: success, failure, pressure, depression, illness, worry, debt. Why? Because if you have a worldly mindset then you can only ever see a human way out: "I must work harder ... I must do this or that ... " That just drives you deeper into despair. If your mind is fixed on God however, you will find a supernatural solution to the problems you face.

The Bible says that Jesus will keep us in perfect peace if our mind is stayed on Him (see Isaiah 26:3). Through Christ, our minds can receive a level of peace and freedom that is completely unattainable by human effort. If we allow our minds to be dwell on carnal things then we will be imprisoned by every circumstance that that comes against us, but if we live with our minds focused on the things of the Spirit, then we will know supernatural peace and protection and will prevail in any circumstance.

Paul challenged his protégé Timothy to have a "pure

conscience" (1 Timothy 3:9) because he knew that the mind was a battleground, and in battle you need a strategy for action – one that will not only win the battle, but also shorten the war. Keeping your mind free of negative, sinful thoughts will help to guard your heart from anything harmful taking root there. Fixing your mind on the things of the Spirit will help you to keep walking steadily in the Spirit.

One of Satan's main strategies against believers is to persuade them to exalt their hearts to the throne of independence, bringing them into direct conflict with God's authority. The enemy wants to trick us into waging war against the convicting power of the Holy Spirit and violate our God-given conscience. Paul described it as a war where we are wrestling invisible forces, power and principalities that are seeking to oppress us. We all face the obvious temptations of the flesh, but the real battle rages in the heart and mind. The devil knows that when the created conscience of man no longer has the ability to retain the values of Christ, then that mind is given over to live in a polluted state and the believer ceases to be effective for the kingdom of God. The enemy of our faith understands that our minds can be maintained in peace and tranquillity *if* they stayed fixed and concentrated on the Lord Jesus Christ.

Who or what has control of your mind today? The things of this world? Selfish ambition? Perhaps even "innocent" desires to accomplish things you want to do? Or have you allowed the Holy Spirit access to your thought life and brought it under submission to Him? If you have then you will know peace. Don't allow circumstances to dictate your life because they are only the frame and not the whole picture of who you are meant to be. Today God wants to paint His love on the canvas of your life. He wants to fill in the blanks; He wants to bring colour to your life. Let Him do it, because *"As a man thinks in his heart, so is he."*

✔ HEALTH CHECKLIST

Points covered in this chapter:

▶ Thoughts turn into beliefs and beliefs create actions. What is in your heart will shape you as a person.

▶ It is what we do with our thoughts that really counts – especially sinful thoughts. Unchecked thoughts have led to the downfall of many ministers of the gospel.

▶ Confession is vital in maintaining a pure mind. What we speak out simply reinforces the beliefs we already hold in our heart. Therefore our "confession" should be positive, declaring the truth of God's Word about ourselves.

▶ When things go wrong in life it is easy to blame our circumstances – either the circumstances that made us who we are (our childhood, the past), or the circumstances surrounding our downfall. Circumstances however are only the symptoms of a deeper problem.

▶ Circumstances are only the "frame" of your life, not the "picture". If your life is in God's hands then all your circumstances are allowed by Him so that He can reveal more of Himself to you.

▶ In Romans 8:4–5 Paul tells us to "fix" our minds on the things of the Spirit. A mind devoid of God can only see human answers to life's problems, but a mind fixed on God will always see a supernatural solution.

"I CAN DO ALL THINGS THROUGH CHRIST WHO STRENGTHENS ME"

Notwithstanding those who suffer from medically diagnosed illnesses, the vast majority of emotional and psychological problems are the effect of damaged self-esteem. People who lack self-esteem tend to feel powerless and live in danger of being ambushed by their own uncontrollable emotions. And yet, Jesus has an answer for all those who feel helpless:

"I can do all things through Christ who strengthens me."
(PHILIPPIANS 4:13 NKJV)

This is no empty platitude, but a very real promise that you will receive divine power and help whenever you need it. The key to this scripture is to examine it in four parts:

1. ***"I can ... "*** So often we refuse to believe that we *can do something* about the predicaments we find ourselves in. That used to be my problem. Because I wasn't able to read until late in my teens, even up to the age of twenty-five I did not believe that I could achieve anything. So I didn't! Once you realise that God desires to enable you to do many things, your perspective changes and a new horizon of possibilities opens up.

2. ***"... do all things ... "*** At that time I would have been pleased to have been able to do just one thing! Yet, through the transforming of my mind through the Word of God and the power of the Holy Spirit, God's creative power gave me the ability to enter into all that Christ had planned for my life. I became one of the leading insurance salesmen in the UK. I managed the finances of 700 top footballers. I became a director of the PFA Financial Management Ltd. I trained and was ordained as a minister, pioneered a church in Solihull with my wife and one other couple, Geoff and Althea Greenaway, and have seen hundreds of people

saved, healed, and filled with the Holy Spirit. I am married to a wonderful wife, Molly, who has stood by me for thirty-five years, and I have had three wonderful children, Ashley, Melanie and Lucy. I also have a granddaughter, eight spiritually adopted children and fourteen adopted grandchildren! I am involved in training leaders throughout the nation and travelling all over the world among many denominations. Why? Because my mind has been transformed by the power of God's love! I don't say these things to brag, but to prove to you that in Christ, "I can do all things." Just watch this space!

3. *"... through Christ ..."* The secret to successful living is to be "in Christ" and to do everything "through Christ". Jesus Christ is our mediator, the One who is able to connect us with God the Father. When we are operating "through Christ" then our mind and emotions are subject to Him and all our life becomes "the Lord's business".

4. *"... who strengthens me."* The psalmist wrote, "I looked to the hills for my help, but it didn't materialise. My help comes from the Lord." Often in life our strength needs to be manifested in our mind and emotions. Physical strength can be built through diet and exercise, but emotional strength comes from encouragement, inspiration and enthusiasm. When we are in Christ and see His power at work in our lives, it encourages and strengthens us. To be mentored by the Lord Jesus and to be led into all truth by the Holy Spirit gives us the stability for life that we need.

So what prevents us from taking hold of this truth and living it out? Our minds have been trained from infancy to believe, "It's too late for me. I had a bad start in life and you just can't teach an old dog new tricks."

Well first of all, you are not a dog! You are a created being made in the likeness of God. You have been given, through Christ Jesus, the opportunity to be born again and to have a new mind – a mind that has already been tried and tested and found to be totally dependable, the mind of Christ. God's Word can wash your carnal, fearful, negative thinking. You can change from your old patterns of behaviour and approach life afresh through Christ. Oh, and by the way, a dog handler informed me that you can teach an old dog new tricks – it just takes a little longer!

NEW TECHNOLOGY, NEW ISOLATION

When 2025 dawns, the medical profession informs us, a greater level of mental instability than ever previously seen awaits us. When my friend and colleague in the ministry, Dr Chris Oyede, trained in psychiatric medicine, the phobias and syndromes common in Western culture were totally alien to his African culture. Mental illness has both universal and local manifestations. The demand in the West for therapy and counselling is insatiable. With traditional Christian values no longer on the agenda of educational and social authorities, and the family unit rapidly disintegrating, a deep spiritual vacuum has been created. The human race has spiritual needs, so their many mental issues will remain unresolved until they are treated in an holistic way. Medical practitioners need to see faith as an essential part of the healing process and not an obstacle. Because of diminishing church attendance, the local doctor has become the "father confessor" for many. But without the ability to give absolution or to point the afflicted towards the faith community, the only option is to prescribe more and more anti-depressants.

Our technological age has forsaken much human inter-action in favour of computer interaction in an online world. Human contact is increasingly being lost. Few phone calls now receive a personal response. Instead, pre-recorded, push-button, computerised messages direct and re-direct you, without you ever speaking to a human! Even if you do manage to get through to the complaints department to tell them about your leaking gas flue in a suburb of Birmingham, you will probably be speaking to someone in a call centre in Delhi!

Children today have bedrooms full of TVs, DVDs, mobile phones, i-Pods and laptops connected to the internet. A new language is now not on the lips of our children, but at their finger tips: text messaging – a short-hand language that I even noticed as a requirement on a job application form recently!

Computer game graphics are now so advanced that fantasy and reality have crossed over or become very blurred. Children get to play in realistic worlds without adults that have no laws, no values and no morality. They are worlds controlled by the individual. In this virtual world all the interaction you need is supplied on screen by entities which you control, yet the heart of the Christian message is *community*, the need for one another, and the love of God being shared. "Don't neglect to meet together," the writer to the Hebrews advised (Hebrews 10:25), because the need for interaction is essential. These days many stay at home and watch church on TV – No! Push-button cyber church must never take the place of the real thing! It's the vulnerability of rubbing shoulders with other believers – those whom you might not naturally choose as friends – that makes your faith real. Mental and emotional instability is caused by isolation and the tendency to blame others for our limitations. Being church together gives us a reality check and helps us to function properly.

THE WAY AHEAD

This book can never cover adequately such a vast subject as mental wellbeing. Each aspect of mental infirmity, its causes and consequences, could warrant a book in its own right. But I wanted to confront the many misconceptions that people have about mental illness and make the link between that and the importance of having a mind renewed by the power of Christ.

I also plead on behalf of those with genuine emotional illnesses that fellow believers would come to a place of greater understanding and compassion. I believe in God's healing power, but what happens to those who want to belong to a Christian church family on equal terms? They must be able to contribute without well-meaning Christians telling them to "Pull yourself together" or asking, "Where's your faith"; or worse still in some charismatic/Pentecostal circles saying, "You have a demon, you need to be delivered."

We have a steward in our church who greets people at the main doors of the sanctuary. He is in his fifties and is

Down Syndrome. He is not there to prove a point, he is there because he is good, faithful, and is serving his Lord and Saviour. We welcome his contribution to the body of Christ.

We all carry emotional baggage with us. The secret of the Christian life is to lay that baggage at Jesus' feet and allow Him to release you from it. If Jesus Christ is the Saviour of the world, then *your world* can be saved. You don't have to be bound by the hurt of the past; Jesus can deal with it today.

Above all, engage your new spiritual nature in Christ and remember that your past is "past". God says to you, "Behold! I make all things new." In the nicest way possible I say to you, "Grow up!" If that hasn't offended you, then this book has had some positive affect!

Till we meet, keep your mind fixed on Him.

NOTES

Chapter 2
1. Joan E. Gadsby, *Addiction by Prescription* (Key Porter Books, 2000), ISBN 1552633349.
2. E. S. Lisansky-Gomberg (1989), "Suicide Risk Among Women with Alcohol Problems", *American Journal on Public Health*.

Chapter 6
1. From the poem "To a Louse" by Robert Burns.
2. "It is well with my soul", words by Horatio G. Spafford, 1873, music by Philip P. Bliss, 1876.

About the Author

David Carr has been involved in the ministry of the Gospel for over thirty years, travelling extensively throughout the world. David is the Senior Minister of the Renewal Christian Centre, Solihull, which he pioneered in 1972 and is now one of the largest charismatic, Spirit-filled churches in the UK.

Renewal is affiliated to the Free Methodist Church of the UK and North America. Prior to this David was an Executive Member of the Elim Pentecostal Church.

As well as being a local pastor for many years, his experience within the world of professional football, where he managed 700 of the country's leading players, has enabled him to relate to people from all walks of life. He is in great demand as a conference speaker both in the UK and abroad and regularly conducts leadership conferences.

David has a strong prophetic ministry and moves in the gifts of the Holy Spirit. Over recent years many signs, wonders and miracles have been apparent during and after the preaching of the Word. Recently there has been an incredible move of the Holy Spirit within the church which has resulted in many healings and an awesome presence of God.

David is married to Molly and has three children, Ashley, Melanie and Lucy.

We hope you enjoyed reading this New Wine book.
For details of other New Wine books
and a range of 2,000 titles from other
Spirit-filled publishers visit our website:
www.newwineministries.co.uk